BY MARTIN HÄUSSERMANN & FRIENDS

E-Bike

A GUIDE TO E-BIKE MODELS, TECHNOLOGY & RIDING ESSENTIALS

VELO press

BOULDER, COLORADO

THE PERFECT
TOOL FOR
URBANITES

THE MODERN,
ECO-FRIENDLY
KID CARRIER

**INTO THE CITY:
COMMUTERS LOVE
THE E-BIKE.**

ENJOY FRESH AIR
AND FAIR SKIES
ALL DAY LONG.

FROM THE AUTHOR

E-biking is wonderful. I say that with the deepest of convictions and after years of enjoyment on bikes of all kinds. I cannot remember exactly when an e-bike first appeared in our garage; what I do know is that my entire family uses e-bikes for myriad reasons—and to many a great benefit. My wife, a doctor, has ridden to work on an e-bike for the past six years. My younger son used to take the bus to school, but after the bus schedule changed, he now uses one of my e-bikes. And my eldest son now loves to take his e-mountain-bike to the trail—sometimes using electric assistance, sometimes not. We all own muscle-powered bikes too, and use them interchangeably.

Not every family is as crazy about bikes as mine, and some have a difficult time finding room for them in their lives and literally in their homes—we do too! Choosing to buy an e-bike might come down to a decision to swap a conventional bike for an e-bike, but other e-bike owners may find they ride their other bikes more often too. Whether or not you can find the right e-bike isn't a question anymore, as the bicycle industry has electrified every type of two-wheeler, and the options continue to expand. From city bike to mountain bike, lightweight road bike to cargo bike—all of them can be fitted with an electric motor. You will find essential information regarding the various types of e-bikes throughout this book.

Don't let anyone tell you that e-bikes are only suitable for older or less athletic people or for commuters and urbanites. That is simply not true. On the contrary, e-bikes help people become more active again—both those who formerly lacked motivation or experience with a bike and those who worried that they might run out of energy before reaching their destination. And on the other side of the spectrum, there are very sport-oriented bikes for fit, experienced cyclists who like to tackle virtually every terrain available—now with electric assistance.

E-bikes open new dimensions to cycling. They extend the distance riders can travel or help riders do more with the endurance they have. You will read about these and other advantages in the very first chapter.

There is a lot more to say, and you will read about much of it on the following pages. I truly hope to convey at least some of my enthusiasm for e-bikes. If you only buy this book as a practical guide, that's great, but please do not just toss it somewhere in the garage . . . use it!

If I may add a final request: please always wear a helmet when cycling, and ride safely; both can save your life.

Enjoy your ride!

CONTENTS

THE
MAGIC OF
THE E-BIKE

E-BIKE WORLD
AN ENGINEERING PIONEER
OPINION

WELCOME TO E-BIKE WORLD

ELECTRIC POWER MAKES RIDING A BIKE EVEN MORE UNIVERSALLY ACCESSIBLE—AND MORE FUN. E-BIKES MAY HAVE BEEN SEEN MERELY AS A NOVELTY SOME YEARS AGO, BUT NOW, JUST ABOUT EVERY POPULAR BIKE MANUFACTURER OFFERS SUPPLEMENTAL-ELECTRIC-POWER MODELS IN ITS LINEUP—IN NEARLY EVERY CATEGORY. FOR MANY, E-BIKES EVEN REPRESENT AN ALTERNATIVE TO DRIVING A CAR, WITH ALL THE FINANCIAL AND ENVIRONMENTAL BENEFITS THAT REPLACEMENT ENTAILS.

TEXT & PHOTOS: MARTIN HÄUSSERMANN

In 1932, the electronics company Philips debuted a bicycle model that included an electric motor. Placed in the middle of the bike's triangular frame, the motor powered the rear wheel via the chain; the battery sat in the bottom of the frame to allow for an optimal center of gravity—just as they often do today. In spite of its sensible design, the Philips Simplex Electric Bike was far ahead of its time—by some 75 years.

The term "e-bike" has been a label for more than one form of vehicle. It was once reserved only for electric mopeds, which are powered solely by an electric motor and do not require any physical effort on the part of the user. But these days, an e-bike is a bicycle driven by pedals with electric assistance. And they have really taken off—not just in the literal sense. In the US, nearly 80 percent more e-bikes were sold in 2018 than in 2017. And so the world, and opportunity, of e-bikes continues to grow.

VARIETY ATTRACTS ALL KINDS OF RIDERS
The reasons behind the grand success story are many; one standout is the enormous variety of models available. There is indeed no bike category today that doesn't have a model also available in an electric version. While only cumbersome, unsophisticated models were available years ago (particularly targeted at making bike riding more accessible for older riders), the e-bike world is now much more vibrant and geared toward riders young and old: with hip urban bikes, mountain bikes, cargo bikes, and even racing bikes with electric drive assistance. E-bikes have done away with the "old fogy" image and instead have become a symbol of a modern, eco-friendly lifestyle.

LEAVE THE TRAFFIC BEHIND
In an age where traffic jams have become the norm and emissions from gas-burning auto–mobiles cause public health and environmental problems, many have started to think differently. The number of people commuting from home to work on a bike is steadily increasing. For short distances through the city, a bike already can't be beat, and the parking convenience alone is usually much better than for a car! In the event that you have to pick up more than a few things from the store, or the kids need to be taken to and from school, a bike trailer or a cargo bike is an easy solution. Of course, all these things are also possible on a bike without electric drive assistance. But having an electric wind at your back helps defeat any hesitations of making the

In cities, the e-bike reigns supreme over other modes of transportation.

CONQUER YOUR WORLD WITH AN ELECTRIC WIND AT YOUR BACK.

First to day care, then grocery shopping. With an e-cargo-bike, even everyday errands become an adventure.

effort to pedal rather than drive. When a bike commute seems too long, an e-bike commute easily becomes feasible. Riding an e-bike to an appointment means you won't arrive completely drenched in sweat, which is an especially important argument for topographically challenging cities like Seattle or San Francisco.

Even the longstanding tradition of "earning your turns" among athletic mountain bikers and roadies is turning the corner to electrification. A motor helps level the playing field among cycling friends out for a fun ride, as you'll learn from a few stories told in these pages. A stronger cyclist can ride to their heart's content on a traditional bicycle, regardless of road or riding conditions, and a weaker or less experienced cyclist will still be able to keep up with the help of the motor assistance. This enables couples or groups of differing abilities to go on cycling trips that will be enjoyable for everyone. For some young or young-at-heart mountain bikers who have no trouble with difficult terrain, the motor just accelerates the fun. They love to ride steep, challenging singletrack trails and downhills— the more the better. On the way to the next slope, it's simple: use a motor instead of hiking up or taking the chairlift.

The e-fat-bike is a type of e-MTB that maintains grip even on the loosest surfaces.

Even cities dominated by cars are making room for bikes.

NEW PERSPECTIVES

My esteemed colleague Gunnar Fehlau, who pops up here and there in this book and who also is the proud owner of an impressive number of bikes, once told me, "A new bicycle piques my interest when it opens new possibilities and perspectives for me." An e-bike can do that, no doubt, even if it's just on a leisurely Sunday ride, spontaneously going left or right off the planned route. The motor is there to help get you home safely in a pinch too. A motor also encourages older people or people who are aiming to lose some weight to get back in the saddle without

any insecurity. They don't need to be afraid of riding the next steep hill or getting out of breath, and they'll be doing something good for their health. After spending some time building up their conditioning on the e-bike, people who might have originally needed the motor for assistance may even find themselves reducing the level of motor support or turning it off altogether. The argument of "I am way too young to need an e-bike" is really something of the past. What do we say to the skeptics? Get on and try it! Without a doubt, after their test ride they won't be able to wipe the grin from their face.

NECESSITY, THE MOTHER OF INVENTION

ELECTRICAL ENGINEER BERNHARD SPRENGER USED AUTOMOBILE PARTS TO BUILD AN EARLY ITERATION OF AN E-BIKE IN 1983, EARNING NO RECOGNITION FOR A TRUE LEAP IN BIKE ENGINEERING. THE TIME WAS JUST NOT YET RIGHT. STILL, HIS STORY OF INNOVATION IS ONE THAT WE CAN IDENTIFY WITH TODAY, SHARING IN THE JOY OF RIDING A BIKE WITH A LITTLE ASSISTANCE—NO MATTER THE REASON.

TEXT & PHOTOS: MARTIN HÄUSSERMANN

With a friendly smile and sparkling eyes, Bernhard Sprenger welcomed me into his garage, saying, "Welcome to my tinkering cave." The 77-year-old retiree's garage is full of tools, as well as electrical measurement and charging devices. There is no doubt that an electrical engineer is busy here—and no doubt that he is also a longtime e-bike fan. Even before we begin speaking about his little piece of history, Sprenger examined my own e-bike, the Riese & Müller Delite hybrid I rode to our meeting. Fittingly, the Delite was bedecked with a Bosch e-bike transmission; after all, that's the company for which he once worked. The transmission features a double-battery system and Nyon display with integrated GPS. The technology I used to arrive at his home serves as a monument to this man's role in developing the e-bike.

Sprenger worked in the electronics and research and development departments at Bosch. His specialty was in high-voltage meters for automobile ignitions. Bosch made a name for itself early in the company's history as a supplier to car manufacturers, which remains an important part of the company's business.

Back in Sprenger's day, no one showed any interest in e-bikes. But he continued to dream up designs for an electric-powered bike. His career eventually led him to a position at the Bosch development facility, where a bicycle path leading up to a plateau consisted of just under 500 feet of climbing through a forest, making for a pretty steep climb. "Riding a bike to work was fun for me, but I wanted to make it a little easier so that I didn't arrive to work all sweaty," explained Sprenger. Thus began his efforts to transform an old bike that he had received while in grade school into an e-bike.

It was no easy undertaking, as e-bike trans–missions did not yet exist, and neither did the other parts needed to complete the modifications for the bicycle. So this natural-born tinkerer reached for anything that was available and adaptable to his design. For the power supply, he chose a device used for lighting in a gutted VW bug. In the car, it generated 180 W at 6 volts. However, because Sprenger had decided on a 12-volt battery, he was able to generate even more power from it, already entering the range of power offered by today's e-bikes.

Due to weight concerns, he initially chose to use a motorcycle battery, but its capacity proved insufficient: "The battery was empty halfway into my commute." So he hung a more powerful car

Bosch engineer Bernhard Sprenger used car parts to build his own e-bike 25 years ago.

A MOTORCYCLE
BATTERY WAS
LIGHTER, BUT IT
DRAINED FAR
TOO QUICKLY.

AT THAT TIME, PEOPLE WERE STILL OF THE OPINION THAT BICYCLES DIDN'T NEED MOTORS.

Sprenger was resourceful. He used a car alternator for the propulsion system, and a car fog light provided the necessary light at night.

Multiple gears made riding uphill easy. A device (measuring amperes) on the handlebars displayed the battery charge.

battery within the main triangle of the frame. Everything he secured to the frame was held by straps: "It wouldn't have been a good idea to drill into the frame's tubes because the frame's integrity would have been compromised." The engineer was then barely able to make it to work because the battery provided almost exactly 3 miles of assist.

Compared to the maximum power generated by e-bikes today, Sprenger's solution provided a relatively measly amount of power. But it was enough for him. And he had enough spare power to play a car stereo along the way. He added a front light—taken from the Bosch automotive fog light collection—after he fell along that forest path one winter day due to poor visibility.

Sprenger connected roller wheels from old office chairs to an alternator. With the flick of a switch, the roller wheels applied power by friction to the rear wheel, which worked best in dry conditions, and helped push the engineer up the hill toward work at a speed of 12 mph. The roller wheels also served as a transmission brake on the way home, thereby putting back a little electricity in the battery by charging it. "When it snowed or rained, the roller wheels had less purchase on the tire, so I had to pedal harder," pointed out the still-fit retiree. Sprenger never noticed additional wear to the rear tire.

The battery, on the other hand, was worn out after 220 charging cycles: "So I had to buy myself a new one every year."

He rode from his home up to the hilltop office for seven years. At work, however, no one showed any interest in his idea. He suggested that the company pursue his idea of an electric bike and developed technical drawings of the concept, but the company declined: "In those days, people thought of bikes as sporting goods that needed no motor," explained Sprenger.

After Bosch's success in the e-bike market, Sprenger tried to make suggestions to the company a second time—to which he received a prompt answer. Claus Fleischer, director of Bosch eBike Systems, responded to Sprenger personally, writing him by hand: "Your invention was probably just too ahead of its time. A great idea is followed by a long path, and yours will be seen as a success story." Sprenger received a 250 euro gift certificate for a local bike shop, where he used it to purchase a helmet and a lock for his current e-bike, which does not feature a Bosch system: "Such a bike was too expensive for me at the time," explained Sprenger. Looking at my Delite again, he brooded: "Having such a bike would be awesome." And for a Bosch e-bike pioneer, it would be fitting.

OPINION

E-RESPONSIBILITY ON THE TRAILS

THE ELECTRIC MOUNTAIN BIKE IS A HIGHLY CAPABLE MACHINE THAT CAN BRING A LOT OF JOY TO A RIDER. IT'S ALLOWED ON MORE TRAILS IN EUROPE, BUT EVEN THERE, IT REMAINS A POINT OF CONTENTION. THAT NEEDS TO CHANGE, SAYS H. DAVID KOSSMANN, JOURNALIST AND E-MTBER.

TEXT: H. DAVID KOSSMANN. PHOTOS: *BIKE NEWS SERVICE* (PRESSEDIENST-FAHRRAD)

"E-mountain-bike riders are just lazy slackers. They're ruining trails and have no etiquette." "If you can't get up the mountain under your own steam . . . " These comments have appeared in more than one online discussion or on the side of the trail post-ride. What can we do to come together as cyclists and remove the tension between riders who enjoy the e-MTB and those who don't?

AN EMOTIONAL DISCUSSION

I am both astounded and confused by how emotionally loaded the topic is. The rejection of e-bikes that is gaining traction in comments sections and forum threads is shocking. How has such black-and-white thinking become so rampant? I recognize the parallels between these sentiments and conversation about topics in our society: fronts are established, differences are emphasized, and unsubstantiated fears are stirred up.

When it comes down to it, though, we all just want the same thing: fun riding bikes in the mountains and in the woods.

These fiery speeches against the new are just as predictable as they are nonsensical in retrospect.

Nearly every technological advancement in cycling has been met with vehement resistance—and then, it's normalized. Why draw a line in the sand when it comes to motors, while other developments are welcomed with open arms? What's the use of making the motor into the bogeyman, especially among brothers and sisters in spirit? No one is losing anything. What especially gets me is the ignorance: Many of the so-called haters have never even sat on an e-MTB and experienced how to move with it. Some aren't even familiar with the concept of pedal assist, and they think e-bikes are actually motorcycles with a throttle.

FINDING COMMON GROUND

I've found that many land managers, environmental organizations, and hikers don't care whether we ride with or without a motor. An e-MTB does no more harm to the trails and forest than a normal bike. To them, it's simply important that we not behave like a bull in a china shop—shouldn't that also be important to us?

There are, by the way, plenty of examples of bikers with and without the extra wattage happily riding together. So, why not remind ourselves of

H. David Kossmann doesn't just ride an e-MTB; he also enjoys riding a nonmotorized singlespeed bike.

WHEN IT COMES DOWN TO IT, WE ALL JUST WANT THE SAME THING: FUN RIDING BIKES IN THE WOODS.

Both in the woods and in life, common courtesy is our basic responsibility, whether we have a motor or not.

the things we have in common and concentrate our efforts that way? There are already many of us, and our numbers are growing steadily. Some of us enjoy using suspension, some prefer to ride singlespeed, some brag about their total elevation gain, some would rather ride the chairlift, and still others will expend serious energy biking to the wildest, off-the-map places. Mountain biking has never been so socially acceptable, or easier. So, it's only natural that our growing numbers will also prove problematic in certain areas. There are indeed some crowded trails out there. But it is possible to address those problems head-on—both tourism and local industries have a vested interest in doing so. If not, then we are all faced with an important task—one that could stand a lot more careful thought, energy, and elbow grease.

Note: By "e-MTB" I mean the commercially available all-terrain e-bikes that do not provide motor assistance above 20 mph and are actually only faster than regular mountain bikes when traveling uphill. I am not referring to motorized dirt bikes, mopeds, customized e-bikes, or any other two-wheeler that goes 50 mph (80 kmh) and tears up the woods.

E-BIKE TECHNOLOGY

TOURING BIKES

Originally conceived of as the ideal bike for long-distance journeys, touring bikes have long established themselves as the go-to choice for everyday cycling. The use of electric motors on touring bikes actually complements their original intended use, as they ultimately expand just how far the rider can go.

You could say they're the Swiss Army knife of e-bikes. They are available in all the popular frame styles: a step-through, a "diamond frame" with a relatively high top tube, and even a low-step style for easiest access.

EQUIPPED FOR EVERYDAY USE

A fully equipped everyday bike typically includes a light, fenders, a rear luggage rack, and a kickstand. Those who enjoy longer trips may appreciate having a rear-mounted kickstand, which helps stabilize the bicycle when it is fully loaded with luggage. While aluminum continues to be the dominant choice for frame material, customers have the choice between 700c wheels with comparably narrower tires and 27.5-inch tires like those used on some mountain bikes.

Bosch's front-wheel ABS works perfectly. While the rear wheel locks up when braking hard on gravel, the ABS is hard at work up front.

FACTS & FIGURES

Riese & Müller Homage
Price: starting at $6,200
Frame material: aluminum
Tire size: 27.5 inches
Weight: starting at 64 pounds
Maximum total weight: 300 pounds
Motor: mid-drive Bosch Performance CX, 250 W
Battery: Bosch, 36 V, 13.4Ah / 500 Wh
Drivetrain: 11-speed Shimano Deore XT
Brakes: Magura MT4 disc with ABS (Europe only)

This model came
with two batteries
to carry a rider the
extra distance.

IN DETAIL

1
The black box under the headlight houses the
electronic controller and a portion of the Bosch
antilock braking system (ABS).

2
The hydraulic brakes were developed together
by Magura and Bosch. A small sensor is
mounted on the front wheel, next to the
brake disc.

3
To the right of the Bosch Intuvia display, you
can see a smaller display that lets the rider
know when ABS is engaged.

4
The Gates belt drive provides a connection
between the Bosch motor and the Rohloff hub
that is perfect for long distances and easy
to maintain.

A number of other components from mountain bikes, such as sturdy derailleurs, gears, or disc brakes, are also frequently used. Suspension forks are actually standard in this bike category, and especially high-quality models may even offer rear suspension as well. An alternative (or plush complement) to front and rear suspension is suspension under the saddle; a little give under the seat takes the edge off bumpy roads quite effectively.

A PREMIUM BIKE AT A PREMIUM PRICE
The Riese & Müller Homage pictured here is, at first glance, not the archetype of a touring bike, particularly because it features a low-step style frame. But the way that it's outfitted tells

another story entirely. Take the wide 27.5-inch tires (Schwalbe Rock Razor), for example, which in tandem with the full suspension, promise comfort for long-distance riding. And then there's the drivetrain, which combines the Bosch Performance Line CX motor with the electronic 14-gear internal hub from Rohloff (offering a gear range up to 520 percent). The motor and the rear wheel's hub are connected with a low-maintenance Gates belt. Its Magura disc brakes and excellent lighting system together offer maximum safety. The extremely bright Supernova M99 front light (1,250 lumens) makes even the darkest night feel like day. In short, this is a fine, albeit not altogether inexpensive, companion for long-distance bike trips.

CITY BIKES

The term "city bike" does not fully describe the
options here, as this type of bike is well-suited
for far more than just city traffic. Even longer
distances are a breeze with a bike like this, not to
mention the physical health benefits it offers
to commuters. Relatively narrow tires are usually
chosen for these bikes to provide a smooth ride
on city asphalt or otherwise paved country or
rural roads.

A WIDE VARIETY

Modern city e-bikes spend a lot of time on busy
streets, so lighting is very important. Many such
bikes come with standard-issue LED head- and
taillights. Most city e-bikes are also equipped with
a suspension fork. All this is topped off with a
(usually optional) suspension seat post, providing
a comfortable ride even over the roughest
potholes. The majority of city bikes have a mid-
drive design (more detail of motor types begins
on p. 50). When it comes to gears and shifting,

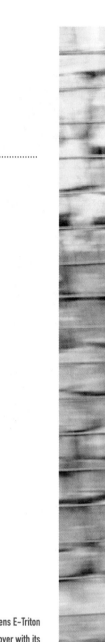

The Stevens E-Triton
won us over with its
superior handling,
high-quality build,
and elegant design.

FACTS & FIGURES

Stevens E-Triton PT 5
Price: starting at €3,500 (only available in Europe)
Frame material: aluminum
Tire size: 700c
Weight: starting at 55 pounds
Maximum total weight: 309 pounds
Motor: mid-drive, Bosch Performance CX, 250 W
Battery: Bosch, 36 V, 13.4 Ah / 500 Wh
Drivetrain: 11-speed Shimano Deore XT
Brakes: Shimano BR-M 6000 disc

We tested the 2018
E-Triton; the 2019
model features only
slight changes.

IN DETAIL

1
The Busch and Müller headlight ensures
optimal visibility, especially at night.
It is mounted deeper on the 2019 models.

2
A high-quality saddle is standard on the
Stevens, but it could also be upgraded with
a suspension seat post.

3
The Bosch PowerTube battery is cleanly
integrated into the sturdy down tube.
A cover protects it from dirt and moisture.

4
The rear light, integrated into the luggage
rack, adds a delicate, elegant look. It is
enhanced by a wide reflector.

variety is the name of the game. Derailleurs are just as available as internal gear hubs. Some of these internal gear hubs (e.g., from Shimano) enable back-pedal braking (otherwise known as coaster brakes), which remains a favorite even with some of the most seasoned e-bike riders. Some bikes with coaster brakes can also be outfitted with disc brakes for additional security. The casual cyclist may also find the automatic shifters from Shimano or NuVinci useful.

AN ELEGANT COMPANION FOR THE WHOLE DAY

For this category we have evaluated and photo–graphed the Stevens E-Triton. What we have here is a visually and technically balanced e-bike, which, after 60 test miles, we can unequivocally recommend. The frame's well-planned geometry and the integrated "in-tube" battery offers premium stability even at high speeds. The Shimano disc brakes are well sized and allow even a loaded bike to come safely to a halt. Outfitted with high-quality components, this e-bike promises a first-class ride and sustained functionality for many years. The bike you see here is the 2018 model; the 2019 model has a few cosmetic upgrades. But the same is true for both models: This bike is an elegant companion, whether you're on your way to work, shopping, or just enjoying a leisurely weekend ride.

E-MTBs

The mountain bike is to cycling what the SUV is to regular cars. It is technically advanced and beloved for its ability to do just about anything, but it is also not always used for its intended purpose. It is not uncommon to see mountain bikes in all stages of customization being ridden around town or even in big cities, fenders and clip-on lamps and all. The basic principle is clear: A mountain bike offers wide, deep-tread tires, is generally outfitted with suspension in either the front fork or both front and rear, and it is built tough. The suspension fork is not only responsible for comfort, it also ensures maximum contact with the trail surface, even in the most challenging terrain.

SPORTY, WITH A MOTOR

Electrification of mountain bikes is a hot topic, but we are heading that way (and in Europe, they're deeper into this transition to pedal-assist mountain biking); it's something many purists consider almost sacrilege. The same could be said for carbon frames back in the day though. Any type of innovation runs the risk of being regarded with suspicion or considered unathletic. When it comes to mountain biking, however, motors don't just bring relief to the hearts, lungs, and legs; they also bring bikers all sorts of new opportunities. Thanks to motors, you're no

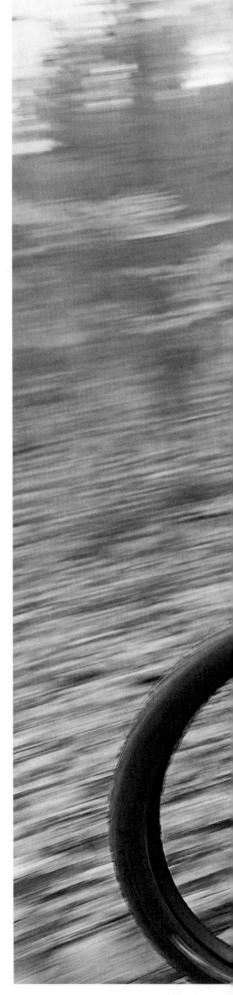

The Scott Genius is especially fun to ride when it's in its element—off-road and at high elevation.

FACTS & FIGURES

Scott Genius eRide 900 Tuned
Price: starting at $7,499
Frame material: aluminum
Tire size: 29 inches (optionally 27.5 inches)
Weight: 52 pounds
Maximum total weight: 282 pounds
Motor: mid-drive, Shimano Steps E8000, 250 W
Battery: Shimano, 36 V, 500 Wh
Drivetrain: 12-speed SRAM X01 Eagle
Brakes: Shimano BR-M 8020 XT disc

IN DETAIL

1
The left hand doesn't just control the level
of assistance from the motor; the upper lever
also controls the suspension travel.

2
The Shimano display is compact and provides
real-time updates about the battery charge,
the selected motor assistance, and speed.

3
The Shimano battery is integrated into
the down tube and can be removed quickly.
A cover protects the battery.

4
The Shimano Steps E8000 was specially
developed for use in e-mountain-bikes.
An additional plastic covering protects
the crank case.

The Scott Genius eRide has many strengths, and few weaknesses. If you're looking for a dynamic bike that's fun to ride, look here.

longer restricted to riding that steep trail only downhill—you can tackle it uphill as well. Some folks refer to this as "uphill flow."

The e-MTB has evolved closely with the analogue mountain bike, but the added weight of a motor and battery has made the e-MTB significantly heavier. The essentials remain the same though: You have to actively pedal, and you have to navigate you and your bike through challenging terrain, bumps, rocks, roots, and dips. E-mountain-biking is indeed a sport.

ALL-TERRAIN ALL-ROUNDER

There are solid e-mountain-bikes to be had for as little as $2,700. We specifically chose to showcase a top-of-the-line model here so we could demonstrate all that's available, knowing full well that only the die-hard fans and connoisseurs would be willing to shell out that much. Scott charges around $7,000 for the Genius eRide 900 Tuned. That price, however, delivers one of the most versatile all-mountain e-bikes on the market. Its versatility is notable, among other things, by the way it is constructed, able to accommodate two wheel sizes (either 27.5 or 29 inches) without changing the geometry. At the core of the Genius is its unique eRide alloy frame with adjustable travel (with a maximum of 150 mm) and the ability to adjust the assist response. It also features the Shimano Steps E8000 e-bike system, which was specifically developed for e-MTBs.

E-ROAD-BIKES

E-road-bikes take the sleek, lightweight, zippy characteristics of traditional road bikes and elevate them to a new level. Road bikes were made to go fast and far while offering a cyclist comfortable, efficient position for hours and hours in the saddle. A pedal-assist road bike can help you tackle the most epic rides on asphalt, especially showing its worth in the highest mountain passes or toughest headwinds.

A MOTOR AS EMERGENCY ASSISTANCE

The definition of a road bike is pretty clear-cut: narrow tires on 700c rims, characteristic drop handlebars, and no unnecessary accessories that don't directly improve or impact its performance on the road. These bikes are driving machines, period. But this hard definition is starting to soften more and more. Tires have become wider, allowing the rider to occasionally turn off the pavement and try a dirt or gravel road. Disc brakes, customarily used on mountain bikes, are finding their way onto road bikes. Even the e-motor is catching the attention of a few fans here and there. In this case, though, the electric motor appears to be treated more as a last-resort assistance in certain situations, such as a particularly tough mountain or when a ride went faster or farther than planned, rather than something to be used permanently. For this reason, the Paralane[2] (Parlane Squared) uses a less intrusive type

Even if you remove the motor-battery unit, the Focus Paralane[2] still performs like a full-fledged road bike on its own.

FACTS & FIGURES

Focus Paralane[2] 9.8
Price: starting at €6,399 (only available in Europe)
Frame material: carbon
Tire size: 700c
Weight: 28 pounds
Maximum total weight: 265 pounds
Motor: Fazua Evation (mid-drive, integrated battery and motor)
Battery: Fazua Evation, 250 Wh
Drivetrain: 11-speed Shimano Ultegra Di2
Brakes: Shimano Ultegra R8020 disc

The Paralane² battery
and motor are
barely noticeable . . .
as it should be on a
high-performance
road bike.

IN DETAIL

1
The electronic Shimano Ultegra Di2 is steered
(and braked) with a classic brake-shift lever.

2
The small controller on the handlebars
operates the three-level assistance, denoted
by color-coded LEDs.

3
The entire battery-motor unit needs to be
completely removed for charging. The green
illuminated diodes indicate the battery
charge level.

4
The flange provides the connection between
the motor and the bottom bracket gear
system. If the motor is removed, a lid covers
the hole.

of motor technology than many standard mid-drives. It features a transmission that, when turned off, doesn't create any resistance to the muscle-powered turning of the cranks, which can significantly disrupt or hinder the usual zippy, efficient feel of a road bike. On the Paralane² the Spanish manufacturer ebikemotion's compact rear wheel motor helps keep this lively feeling intact.

ADD POWER TO A PERFECT RIDE

An alternative to the more common motors appears on the Focus Paralane², which uses a Fazua battery and motor. The German-made motor offers 250 W of average or continuous power and a maximum of 400 W (occurring in brief accelerations), with a maximum assisted

speed of 15 mph. This motor is designed such that, when not engaged, it does not generate any resistance to your own pedaling, saving you valuable energy. Fazua integrates the motor and battery into a unified unit housed in the down tube. If, at some point, a rider would prefer to forego the motor assistance and save themselves a few pounds of added weight, it is easy to simply remove the battery and motor and replace it with a specially designed cover. Suddenly, a very light and capable traditional road bike is in your hands. After two weeks of test-riding, we can conclude: It's a lot of fun, albeit expensive. Of the available Focus models, the Paralane² is the most basic and starts at a cost of $5,700; the top model costs double that.

E-CARGO-BIKES ARE
SOLVING ALL SORTS
OF TRANSPORTATION
DILEMMAS IN
BIG CITIES.

SPECIALTY BIKES

No bicycle has been able to escape the spread of electrification. Even the low-lying recumbent bicycles, tricycles, compact folding bicycles, and the ever more popular cargo bikes are all available with motors.

RECUMBENTS

Recumbent bicycles have offered riders a comfortable alternative to the classic cycling position since the 1980s, and they have only grown in popularity since then. Especially practical is the three-wheeled variety, which won't tip over and which we found to offer a lot of fun and riding pleasure—especially when supported by a motor. A pedal-assist motor is particularly helpful while riding uphill, as the recumbent bicycle rider (unlike an upright cyclist) is unable to pedal standing up. For this reason, German manufacturer HP Velotechnik offers a motorized version of every model it makes. The HP Velotechnik's top model, the Scorpion 26, features full suspension and axle-pivot steering, with all the latest advancements, including a blinker and a brake light. We tested the Scorpion with a hub motor from Go SwissDrive, which is currently out of production but still available through HP Velotechnik.

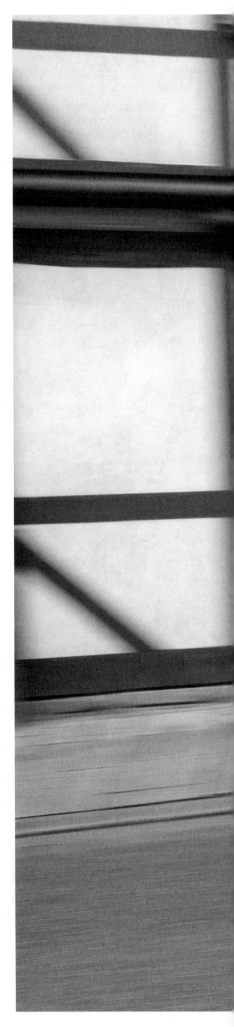

The Scorpion 26 provides a comfortable and fast ride.

RECUMBENTS & TRIKES

HP Velotechnik Scorpion 26
Price: starting at $8,490
Frame material: aluminum
Tire size: rear 26 inches, front 20 inches
Weight: starting at 82 pounds
Maximum total weight: 309 pounds
Motor: Go SwissDrive rear motor, 250 W; alternative: mid-drive Shimano E5000 or E8000
Battery: Go SwissDrive 636 Wh; Bosch 500 Wh
Drivetrain: 11-speed Shimano Deore XT
Brakes: Magura disc

It's a piece of cake folding and unfolding the Brompton Electric. The battery fits in the handlebar bag.

FOLDING E-BIKES

Brompton Electric
Price: starting at $3,499
Frame material: aluminum
Tire size: 16 inches
Weight: 37 pounds
Maximum total weight: 236 pounds
Motor: Brompton front hub, 250 W
Battery: Brompton, 36 V, 300 Wh
Drivetrain: 2-speed hub, Sturmey-Archer
   (with option for 6 gears)
Brakes: Brompton rim brakes

FOLDING BIKES

Want to always have your bicycle with you? Unfortunately, that's not always an option with traditional models. But a folding bike fits in your trunk, and you can take it with you on the bus or train. Brompton was the first to offer a motorized folding bike. The Brompton Electric (from $3,499) has a front hub motor, and the battery is located in a bag that attaches at the handlebar. In all other aspects it's no different from its unmotorized counterpart. Fans of the mid-drive motor should look for folding bikes from manufacturers Tern and Bafang, which use Bosch motors.

A pack mule on two or three wheels can haul nearly any load, thanks to electric power. Left, the Transporter from Riese & Müller.

CARGO BIKES

Riese & Müller Packster 80 Touring
Price: starting at $6,690
Frame material: aluminum
Tire size: rear 27.5 inches, front 20 inches
Weight: starting at 80 pounds
Maximum total weight: 440 pounds
Motor: mid-drive, Bosch Performance Line CX, 250 W
Battery: Bosch, 36 V, 500 Wh
Drivetrain: 11-speed Shimano Deore XT
Brakes: Tektro disc

CARGO BIKES

Cargo bikes continue to grow in popularity with people who have a regular need to transport larger loads. Most cargo bikes are built to transport goods, but they can also be outfitted with an additional mechanism for transporting children. There are also a wide variety of build styles—cargo can be carried either in front of or behind the rider, and in addition to many two-wheeled models, there are also a number of three-wheeled models available. What all cargo bikes have in common are very stable frames, roomy luggage racks, and occasionally very long wheelbases. Unlike cars, they facilitate large-load transportation without the added worry of finding a parking place, harming the environment, or high gas prices. Electric motors bring a welcome

added level of support for the rider, especially when it comes to starting from a standstill, but also when riding uphill. A motor can be very beneficial for handling a loaded-down bike—and the added weight of a motor is rather insignificant with a cargo bike that is already heavy in its own right. Both the Bullitt and the Packster from Riese & Müller are among the most popular e-cargo-bikes. The Packster offers a cargo area length of either 15.5", 23.6", or 31.5". It is positioned low and in front of the driver, which not only makes loading and unloading easier, but also improves (among other things) the handling. Thanks to the support of the Bosch Performance Line CX motor, pedaling through town with a fully loaded (440 pounds) Packster is easy.

INSPIRED DESIGN

TEXT: ANDY READ

Bike builders are faced with the need to accommodate e-bike essentials—batteries, motors, wires, sensors, and controls—and some have viewed this as a chance to reconsider a bicycle's fundamental design. As a result, some e-bikes display a fresh take on what it means to connect two wheels to a cyclist, whether it's in the shape of the frame, fun features, or the user interface.

HOMAGE TO THE MOTORCYCLE

Vintage Electric's e-bikes blend the aesthetics of a storied generation of vehicle design with the latest cycling technology. The Cafe and other models were built starting from scratch, both in the application of the electric components and in designing the overall body of the bike. Taking a note from classic motorcycles of the early- and mid-20th century, Vintage Electric, based in Santa Clara, California, developed an easy-to-ride and particularly eye-catching bike in the Cafe.

Even the small components were thoughtfully designed.

The battery can be charged while on the bike or after it's lifted out with the leather handle.

FACTS & FIGURES

Vintage Electric Cafe
Price: $3,995
Frame material: steel (fork: aluminum)
Tire size: 29 inches
Weight: starting at 53 pounds
Motor: rear hub, 750 W
Battery: 48 V / 500 Wh
Drivetrain: 10-speed Shimano Deore
Brakes: hydraulic disc
Top assisted speed: 28 mph
Charge time: 2 hours

The Cafe's power and aesthetic will have you thinking you're riding a motorcycle from another era.

The electric components were handpicked to offer a smooth ride, easy operation, and reliability. Although the Cafe has a fun appearance, its heft makes it a serious and fast commuter. Its steel frame and aluminum fork were built to handle the high-power output (750 W) of the hub motor. Vintage prefers the use of a hub drive for its simplicity, power, and gentle treatment of the drivetrain. A torque sensor in the bottom bracket provides precise and rapid feedback from the stroke of the pedals to the motor, offering a responsive power delivery and smooth changes in speed. The frame, with its curved top tubes and seat tubes, reminds us that designs of another era are just as relevant today.

The battery compartment is stored in a triangular compartment reminiscent of a motorcycle's engine block; it's removed with the lift of a strap made of leather, a material choice that also appears on the saddle and handlebar grips.

SUBTLE, SLEEK SOPHISTICATION

The VanMoof Electrified S2 was built with inspiration from the heart of the big city: smooth, modern, stylish lines and a quiet paint scheme, head- and taillights built into the top tube, and a security system that can ward off potential bike thieves with loud alarms and lights. Among its most innovative features, the matrix-style display in the top tube reshapes a pattern of tiny LEDs to show battery levels, speed, power level, and security status. No display module sits on the handlebars, further accentuating the sleek design.

The front hub delivers 250–500 W under four settings, with an additional quick burst of speed engaged by the click of the boost button. The internally shifting 2-speed drivetrain is enough for most urban topography.

Electronic controls don't just appear on the bike. A smartphone or watch loaded with the VanMoof app allows you to control speed settings, choose lighting options, and set security functions.

VanMoof set out to build the battery compartment so that it's barely noticeable, placed wholly within the shape of the down tube. The front hub motor is inconspicuous, too, as the rear hub is sized similarly to the front. All of these elements are expressions of the Amsterdam, Netherlands, company's belief that a bike design can be pushed into the future. You can visit its shops in several large cities around the world (and shipping is available).

Modern, simple lines almost hide the sophistication of design.

FACTS & FIGURES

VanMoof Electrified S2
Price: starting at $3,398
Frame material: aluminum
Tire size: 700c
Weight: starting at 41 pounds
Motor: front hub, 250–500 W
Battery: 36 V / 504 Wh
Drivetrain: 2-speed, internal-shifting front hub, belt-drive
Brakes: mechanical disc
Top assisted speed: 20 mph

The speaker and rear light are seamlessly integrated into the top tube. Right: A matrix display shows a variety of messages, such as the status of the bike lock system.

E-BIKE CLASSIFICATION & THE RULES OF THE ROAD

AS YOU EXPLORE THE KIND OF E-BIKE YOU'D LIKE TO RIDE, IT'S IMPORTANT TO UNDERSTAND HOW E-BIKES ARE CLASSIFIED IN THE US. THE BIKE'S CHARACTERISTICS MIGHT DETERMINE WHERE YOU CAN AND CANNOT RIDE IT (ALTHOUGH, AS YOU'LL SEE, MOST E-BIKES ARE TREATED AS BICYCLES AND THEREFORE PERMITTED ON THE ROAD).

TEXT: MORGAN LOMMELE
PHOTOS: PEDEGO

E-bikes have been federally regulated since 2002. The US government—in this case, the Consumer Product Safety Commission (CPSC)—decides what can be sold as an e-bike (in contrast, the National Highway Traffic Safety Administration governs mopeds, motorcycles, and motor vehicles). The CPSC defines a "low-speed electric bicycle" as still a bicycle assuming it is a "two- or three-wheeled vehicle with fully operable pedals and an electric motor of less than 750 W (one horsepower), whose maximum speed on a paved level surface, when powered solely by such a motor while ridden by an operator who weighs 170 pounds, is less than 20 mph." The e-bikes we detail in this book fit this definition and are therefore treated as bicycles, which means most other rules of the road apply to them as they do to traditional bikes.

As with other consumer products, federal regulations for e-bikes are limited. They do not specify where e-bikes may be ridden or what rules of the road govern their use. Instead, e-bike rules of the road are a matter of state law. But they vary widely across the country. In many states, e-bikes lack a specific vehicle classification, and it is unclear how they are regulated. They

may be interpreted to fall within terms primarily aimed at combustion engine vehicles, such as mopeds or scooters.

Seeing a need for consistent legislation across state boundaries—in the same way the operator of a car or traditional bicycle would be subject to similar laws from state to state—in 2015 bicycling advocacy groups launched an effort to streamline e-bike definitions and policy. Other emerging technologies, such as Segways, autocycles, and commercial quadricycles, have followed the same path, as new state-traffic laws were created to address the use of these devices on our streets.

The bike industry then came up with a system to define the three classes of e-bikes based on the federal definition of e-bikes, the characteristics of products developed by manufacturers, and European e-bike laws. This system ensures that outdated vehicle regulations are updated to reflect technological advances (e-bikes) and that e-bikes are regulated similarly to traditional bicycles. It also reduces confusion among consumers and retailers regarding their state's e-bike laws, with the goal of encouraging the public to take advantage of all the benefits that e-bikes offer.

In the US, some off-road trail networks are open to e-bikes, but not many. Know the rules before you take to the trails.

The three classes are as follows:
- Class 1: bicycle equipped with a motor that provides assistance only when the rider is pedaling and that ceases to provide assistance when the e-bike reaches 20 mph
- Class 2: bicycle equipped with a throttle-actuated motor that ceases to provide assistance when the e-bike reaches 20 mph
- Class 3: bicycle equipped with a motor that provides assistance only when the rider is pedaling and that ceases to provide assistance when the e-bike reaches 28 mph

For class 1 and class 3 e-bikes, the rider must be pedaling for the motor to be engaged. On class 2 e-bikes, the motor can propel the e-bike without the rider pedaling. As of late 2019, 22 states have incorporated the three-class e-bike system in their traffic codes and regulated them similarly to traditional bicycles. About another 15 states define e-bikes similarly to bikes, but about a dozen states still have outdated laws that lack a specific classification for electric bicycles.

Spend more time outside, whether you're running errands or sightseeing.

The class system has its benefits. By defining class 1, 2, and 3 e-bikes as bicycles (and not motorcycles), e-bikes are not subject to the registration, licensing, or insurance requirements that apply to motor vehicles. The same rules of the road apply to both e-bikes and human-powered bicycles when it comes to speed, proper passing, local traffic laws, speed limits, equipment, and other regulations. The class system also sets in place standards for e-bike equipment and operation. These standards vary slightly from state to state, but in general, helmets are required for riders of class 3 e-bikes, you must be sixteen years old to ride a class 3 e-bike, and all e-bike manufacturers must apply a standard label to each e-bike specifying its type and wattage to help law enforcement agencies identify e-bike classes.

The distinction between the classes of e-bikes also provides greater flexibility at the local level, as local governments can further regulate or prohibit the use of e-bikes in their parks and on paths and trails, according to the class system. Some state and county park systems in California and Colorado, for example, have begun opening traditional MTB trails to one or two classes of e-bikes after conducting on-trail studies and gathering public input. E-bikers should always check with local agencies before venturing onto park trails.

There is an e-bike for everyone, whether you are looking for an additional boost on trails, running errands around town without driving a car, or aiming to shorten your commute. Spend some time learning about the three classes, their purposes, and local regulations; then align your plans for e-biking with these policies so you can find the best bike for you.

MOTORS

MOVING YOU FORWARD

YOU CAN FIND LITERALLY EVERY TYPE OF BICYCLE EQUIPPED WITH A MOTOR,
BUT WHICH ONE IS RIGHT FOR YOU? WHAT ARE THE ADVANTAGES AND
DISADVANTAGES OF A BATTERY MOUNTED IN THE FRAME'S MAIN TRIANGLE RATHER
THAN IN A REAR RACK? WHICH IS BETTER—FRONT- OR REAR-WHEEL DRIVE?
LEARN WHAT MAKES A MOTOR TICK, SO YOU CAN DECIDE
THESE THINGS FOR YOURSELF.

TEXT: MARTIN HÄUSSERMANN & PETER BARZEL

The rising popularity of e-bikes is in part due to the growing variety of options, from bicycle design and function to features and transmission types—otherwise known as drives. In the early days of e-bikes, the first mass-produced models featured "easy access" frames, otherwise known as women's frames or step-throughs. They came with either a motorized hub in the front wheel or a Panasonic motor placed somewhere in the frame. Both types are still available, although front-wheel drives have become less common because although they are inexpensive and easy to add as an upgrade, they don't really offer any other advantages over other transmissions. They provide less traction when riding uphill or on loose surfaces, and they make handling a bit unstable. Today, e-bikes are equipped with many types of well-designed drives—and offer many selling points.

DRIVETRAIN SYSTEMS

Today, the most popular type of drivetrain is mid-drive, or "mid-mounted." Panasonic, once the exclusive supplier to e-bike pioneer Flyer, is still a prominent manufacturer of mid-drive motors. The company has been outsold in the last 10 years by Bosch, who is not only the leader in

the mid-drive category, but is by far the market leader in all forms of e-bike transmissions. Yamaha and Shimano Steps drives are also featured on many bikes, as are transmissions from automotive supplier Brose.

The advantage of the mid-drive setup is rooted in simple physics: the motor is built into the lowest part of the bicycle. Low and centered weight makes for more natural movement on the bike. So if the battery is also built into the main triangle of the frame, rather than on a rear rack, the bike will have a better weight distribution and more secure handling.

Mid-drive motors can also be integrated with coaster brakes, which inexperienced cyclists might appreciate. The only slight disadvantage of mid-drive options is that the chain and cogs wear out faster because both a rider and a motor are putting pressure on the moving parts. The chain, front chainrings, and rear cog set are under greater force and increased stress. New chains are being designed to better handle this increased load though. Still, these beefier chains will still stretch over time and should probably be replaced every 1,250 miles.

Those who find chain care and replacement a hassle or don't want to bother with much

E-bike motors are robust and waterproof and therefore work well on even the toughest mountain bike rides.

Bafang H-600:
Chinese manufacturer
Bafang builds motors
to fit all mounting
positions. Pictured
here is a rear-wheel
hub motor system.

maintenance can go with a belt drive trans-mission. These belts have proven their durability in car engines, where they are under much stress and heavy use. For bikes they offer the same benefits: they are silent, dependable, and maintenance-free (and grease-free). Such belts transfer power from a mid-drive motor to the rear wheel hub or connect a traditional pedal crank to a rear hub motor. More about that later. Dependable yet expensive offerings from manufacturers like Rohloff are now a proven option and are already beloved by commuters and touring cyclists.

Comfort-conscious cyclists tend to go with the infinitely variable and optionally automatic-shifting NuVinci transmission hub. Or they go with the Shimano Steps system, which provides an all-in-one transmission unit that monitors pedaling effort and adjusts power output. And here's something really handy about Shimano Steps: When you stop at a red light, for example, the system automatically shifts into a predetermined lower (easier) gear from which to start riding from a standstill. Then you can get going again without any problem when the light turns green.

Despite the progress and success of mid-drive systems, rear hub motors are still a great option. The latter's big advantage? It puts power right where you need it—in the rear wheel, so the stress on chains and belts is the same as it is with muscle-powered bikes. These systems can also contribute to braking on descents, during which it charges the battery. This regenerative braking system hasn't proven to substantially recharge the battery though, so it doesn't quite extend the distance you can travel. Hub motors can be combined with traditional chain drivetrains but also with modern, e-bike-specific drivetrains, including belt drives.

So that you can take away from this book a good idea of what motor and battery choices are available in the e-bike market today, we will briefly introduce you to the e-bike motor manufacturers we consider to be the best, along with their products.

Bosch mid-drive: This is the most beloved and most widely used e-bike drive system. Pictured here with the navigation-capable Nyon display.

BOSCH

MID-DRIVE TRANSMISSIONS

Bosch is the world leader in e-bike transmissions. As an automotive supplier and electric tools manufacturer, Bosch found electric bike motors to be second nature. Ten years ago, the German company founded a business division dedicated to their development: Bosch eBike Systems. After thoroughly studying the question of how to best power a bicycle, Bosch's answer was a mid-drive motor.

The first generation of Bosch motors was produced in 2011. In 2013, the second generation was introduced, separated into two categories: the Active Line and the Performance Line (the latter being lighter, more integrated, more efficient, and more elegant). The second-generation systems were arranged differently so they could be reduced in size. The newer motor generates less vibration, and its electronics react more quickly due to three sensors that give off a signal 1,000 times per second, making it faster and more sensitive. The sensors monitor the movement of the drivetrain to provide smooth power when the rider shifts gears, thereby reducing the need for supplemental electric assistance and providing easier shifting with less wear. The smaller model spares the system one gear, thereby saving electric energy and improving battery life.

Riders will find the transition between assist and no assist to be smooth thanks to the motor's stand-by mode, which minimizes the resistance from the motor during muscle-powered pedaling.

Yamaha mid-drive: This is the only motor that offers the ability to mount two front chainrings.

The motor-driven gear is housed within the larger gear that is driven by the muscle-powered cranks. This approach has been applied to several models.

The mid-level Active Line offers an option for coaster braking, while the more dynamic Performance Line is available in versions for both 20 mph and the higher-powered 28 mph maximum-assisted speeds.

For e-MTBs, Bosch created another level of electric assistance designed to better determine a rider's needs and provide power in off-road conditions. And Bosch added variety to how information is displayed on the bike, too: along with the well-known, centrally mounted Intuvia display, Bosch now offers the Nyon display with GPS functionality and the very compact, bar-end-mounted Purion display. And beginning in 2019, active cyclists can also make use of the slender Kiox on-board computer.

YAMAHA
MID-DRIVE MOTORS
Yamaha introduced the first mass-produced e-bike in 1993 with its original Power Assist System (PAS), essentially inventing the e-bike category, and then lobbied in Japan and Europe for the category to be officially recognized as a bicycle industry product. That enabled e-bikes, as we now know them, to be sold in international bicycle markets. Until the beginning of the 21st century, Yamaha was a leading

e-bike manufacturer. About a decade ago, Yahama e-bikes had disappeared from the market. Then, twenty years after its first mass-produced e-bike, Yamaha was back in the market with its Next Generation offering.

The Next Generation drivetrain offers the standard three sensors of today's e-bikes, monitoring speed, power, and pedal cadence. The motor is also electronically monitored. At just over seven pounds, it is very lightweight and provides a lot of torque (60 Nm) relative to some other brands (torque is another measure of a motor's ability to deliver power). Additionally, Yamaha makes it possible for two chainrings to be installed—something many mountain bikers can appreciate.

A small control panel next to a handlebar grip makes it easy to turn the system on and off. It also displays how much battery life remains, the level of power assistance engaged, the estimated distance for which it can still provide that assistance, and the bike's speed. This centrally placed control panel, complete with remote control, additionally offers all standard bike computer functionality—even a clock and outside temperature.

SHIMANO STEPS
MID-DRIVE WITH AUTOMATIC TRANSMISSION
In most areas of the bike world, Shimano is a trendsetter. With regard to e-bikes, though, the Japanese manufacturer took its time. When it

Shimano mid-drive: The Japanese bike parts maker currently has three different drive systems on the market.

did jump in, it developed a highly engineered system—typical of Shimano products—called Steps, introducing it in 2014. The system includes a specially designed chain with a surface that generates less friction; it's also intended to handle the increased power output generated by both muscle and motor. Steps offers a series of products: the E5000 and E6000 were developed for city and touring cyclists, and now there is the Steps E6100. Mountain bikers have the choice between the E7000 and the E8000.

As the market leader in bicycle components, Shimano has brought its electronic Di2 shifting to the Steps lineup, meaning small motors change the derailleur's position rather than traditional cables. This high-tech contribution provides

a combination of advantages. An electronic drivetrain does not come out of adjustment and shifts quickly and precisely. The electricity needed for shifting is taken from the battery. The Steps system plays a part when a rider changes gears, too: The electronic shifter sends a signal to the derailleur; the shift is made when muscle power to the pedals is at the least powerful point of rotation. Motor output is reduced at that instant, making for quiet and fast shifting as well as incurring less wear on the components. Shimano plans to introduce a semiautomatic transmission that shifts into the drivetrain's smallest gear when the e-bike comes to a stop so the rider can optimally start riding again.

Brose (left) and
Panasonic (right):
Both companies build
efficient and powerful
mid-drive motors.

BROSE

MID-DRIVE WITH AUTOMATIC TRANSMISSION

After Bosch, Brose was the second German car manufacturer to enter the e-bike market. Brose is an electromechanical company that supplies windows, car lock systems, seat systems, and electric transmissions to more than 80 automobile manufacturers throughout the world. The Brose brand is known for quality and, in particular, quality electromechanics. Both are evident in its e-bike mid-drive offering. A power-steering motor served as the foundation of its first e-bike motor. In 2010, Brose began the development of its e-bike transmission. And in 2013, it introduced its first rideable prototype at the Eurobike bicycle show in Germany.

From that debut to today, a complete product series has spawned, including the Drive C (250 W, 50 Nm), designed for urban e-bike riding; the Drive T, designed for touring bikes; and the sporty Drive S (the latter two offer 250 W, 90 Nm) for mountain bikes. Brose e-bike transmissions are some of the smallest on the market. The most noteworthy characteristic of the system is its two-step transmission, which

provides quiet functionality and easy-to-use on-and-off control. Especially notable is its coasting mode—unlike other brands, the Brose motor provides no resistance when coasting; a Brose-powered e-bike rides like a normal bike when the motor is not engaged.

PANASONIC

MID-DRIVE WITH AUTOMATIC TRANSMISSION

Panasonic was a pioneer of e-bike drivetrains and was the mid-drive market and technology leader before Bosch dominated the category. Panasonic electric motors were best known for powering the bikes of Swiss bike manufacturer Flyer, a role they had for about twenty years.

Panasonic motors proved their robustness and dependability in everyday use, as well as in e-bike rental, where bikes can really take a beating. Panasonic continued to develop its motor technology over the years and in 2015 introduced a 36-volt motor that made the then-standard 26-volt system obsolete.

The new model contained a few distinct upgrades. First, the greater power capacity opened new doors in the e-bike market—even

SR Suntour hub drive: Motors set within the wheels place the power right where it needs to be.

though the 26-volt system was more than sufficient for comfort and everyday use. Second, the motor drives the chainring directly, doing away with the need for an additional motor cog in the drivetrain and thereby eliminating a source of additional wear in the older system. Third, the motor was adapted to provide assist at higher cadences, as high as 85 revolutions per minute (RPM), an attractive feature for more athletic or more experienced e-bikers who are comfortable pedaling at this moderately high cadence.

In addition to the handlebar-mounted control switch, the Panasonic system offers an illuminated display unit that performs common cycling computer functions and contains a USB port for connections to smartphones, GPS units, and other electronic devices.

The 36 V X0 motor is available in three versions; one of those is specially designed for mountain bikes. New for the 2018/2019 season, the GX0 was introduced with the same 90 Nm torque capacity as its predecessor, which continues to be available.

REAR HUB DRIVE
Cyclists might first think of suspension forks when they hear the name SR Suntour, but the company also produces other components, including e-bike hub motors. SR Suntour's performance hub drive system is featured on e-bikes across several brands. This brushless motor offers four assist levels: eco, tour, climb, and sport. SR Suntour's ATS (Active Torque Sensor) constantly monitors speed, cadence, and torque to best respond to your pedaling, which results in a smooth power delivery to match your own effort.

The motor and sensor, comprising what the company calls the Human Electro Synergy Components (HESC), ensure that the pedaling motion is most natural and predictable. The sensor works to avoid the jerky accelerations that some other motors might offer when you begin pedaling quickly. The motor's continuous power of 250 W (with an instantaneous peak power of 400 W), brings the rider up to the maximum assisted speed of 20 mph.

LEARN TO MASTER YOUR E-BIKE'S DRIVETRAIN TO GET THE MOST OUT OF IT.

The IZIP E3 TRLZ
features the SR Suntour
hub drive, which
fits unobtrusively
as it's about the
same diameter as
the brake rotor.

Bafang mid-drive: Bafang offers a selection of drive-system kits to add to traditional bikes, but they also appear on some complete e-bikes.

BAFANG

MID-DRIVE MOTORS & HUB MOTORS FOR FRONT & REAR WHEELS

Bafang is a Chinese electric-drive manufacturer, operating in the European and US markets, as well as in China. The company has been developing e-mobility vehicle components and complete systems for the past 10 years. In the beginning, Bafang was considered merely a cheap brand, yet the company continued to develop its products and has now shed that reputation. Bafang offers mid-drive systems in several variations as well as hub motors for front and rear wheels.

Among its current lineup, Bafang offers three mid-drive systems. One is the M420 for city and touring e-bikes, which is a further development of the M400 systems (formerly known as Max Drive). The new version functions at a reported capacity of 250 W with a maximum torque of 80 Nm, offering an assisted speed of up to 15 mph (25 kph).

The M500 system, for mountain bikes, provides a reported capacity of 250 W and a maximum torque of 96 Nm. The motor can be paired with either a single or double chainring (a single 44-tooth chainring or a 34/50 double

configuration). That makes for an overall weight of less than 10 pounds for the entire system, including the display and control unit.

Bafang's hub motors, the Mini-Hub front-wheel drive and Mini-Hub rear-wheel drive, are appropriate for casual-use e-bikes and quick trips needing a little assistance. The lightest system, weighing a mere 3.75 pounds for the front hub version, is small in stature as well (front and rear hubs share a diameter of 100 mm); it provides a maximum torque of up to 45 Nm and is designed to provide initial acceleration and ascending assistance as opposed to serving as a permanent drive system.

BATTERIES

TO GO FAR, YOU'LL NEED A GOOD CHARGE

WITHOUT ELECTRICITY, EVEN THE BEST E-BIKE MOTOR IS USELESS. THAT IS WHY AN E-BIKER SHOULD ALWAYS PAY ATTENTION TO THE BIKE'S BATTERY LEVEL. TREAT YOUR BATTERY WELL AND IT WILL RETURN THE FAVOR.

TEXT: MARTIN HÄUSSERMANN

E-bike motors are powered by lithium-ion batteries. This type of battery has been around since the 1970s; today, it's the first choice in solar-energy storage and electric vehicles, among other cutting-edge applications. These batteries will only continue to improve—and add more fun to your e-bike ride. Regardless of the brand or model of your e-bike, it will help to understand a bit more about the power source of your ride so you can take good care of it and enjoy your ride to the fullest.

The battery compartment has long been the telltale sign that a bike is an e-bike. Whether it is mounted to the rear rack, seat tube, or down tube, the black or gray case is always prominent. That's changing though. In 2016, Shimano began to hide its battery within the frame—usually flush in a space in the down tube. In the following year, Bosch, then Bafang, quickly followed suit, offering what is referred to as an "in-tube battery." This design is popular with e-bike owners because it makes for a more elegant frame design and also because it makes an e-bike less recognizable as such, warding off the temptation of theft. You'll see integrated battery storage in other bikes pictured in these pages, such as the VanMoof and Scott.

HANDLE WITH CARE

E-bike batteries require remarkably little maintenance if you do a few things to take good care of them. A sudden direct impact, such as being dropped onto a hard surface, is never good for them. Be sure to examine the battery after any direct hit or if you crash or drop the bike, even if it's not clear whether the battery was hit directly. Take the e-bike to a qualified dealer or mechanic who can discern whether the battery pack is damaged.

HOLDING A CHARGE

Batteries will gradually lose their capacity to hold a charge. An average e-biker need not worry, though: High-quality e-bike batteries, depending on the model, are normally expected to last 500 to 1,000 charging cycles. Conservatively estimated, the average distance one can travel with a fully charged battery is 25 miles, so you can expect to have a battery life span of 12,500 to 25,000 miles. Bosch states that after 500 charging cycles, a battery should have 70 percent the capacity it had when brand-new. That battery is still useful, but it will tend to drain faster, and it will need to be charged more frequently. For shorter distances, this gradual drop in storage

Batteries that are integrated into the bike frame are the latest trend. They allow new directions in aesthetics and construction.

The in-tube battery is hidden behind a cover. It is easily removed for charging.

isn't a problem, but longer rides could prove more frustrating. If this is the case for you, it's worth a visit to a qualified shop. A certified mechanic can test the battery and replace it, which can be costly (but worth it): Battery replacement can run $500 to $800. But you'll gain back the greatest range the battery can offer.

It is possible to find less expensive ways to revive a battery, such as replacing only certain, worn-out subcomponents of a battery with parts found online. However, I advise against taking apart a battery, as correct interaction between the battery pack itself and the electronics of the battery management system cannot be guaranteed.

BATTERY WEAR

Battery wear is normal, but there are ways to minimize it. One tip is to charge batteries at room temperature rather than in very cold or hot temperatures, such as in a garage during the cold of winter or the heat of summer. To make it easier to charge batteries at the right temperature, many manufacturers have designed them to be removeable and easy to carry. It is also recommended to avoid letting a battery run completely out of charge; a battery should be fully charged regularly. In fact, there is no harm in charging the battery after every ride, as there is no risk of the infamous memory effect with lithium-ion batteries. (This phenomenon,

Neoprene covers protect e-bike batteries from winter's cold.

seen in nickel-based batteries, occurs when a battery is charged before it's fully empty and cannot reach a full charge again.)

For those who do not have time for long charging times or who regularly travel many miles in one trip, it makes sense to have a second battery. Riese & Müller, for example, offers an integrated two-battery system that increases a motor's range considerably. The company's DualBattery Technology places a second, full-size battery within the bike frame, in a position that is designed to minimize any compromise to the bike's stability. Other options may be putting a second, charged battery in a bike bag or backpack; in that case, be sure to protect the

battery from cold as well as physical damage. Consider using a special e-bike bag like those offered by cycling bag specialist Ortlieb.

COLD-WEATHER RIDING

Riding a bike in the winter does require a little more consideration. When a battery isn't used frequently in colder temperatures, the ions don't move as freely, therefore requiring more energy to power the motor. The battery will then lose its charge sooner. Colder temperatures can cut an e-bike's range in half, which is why e-bikers should use an insulated battery cover in winter conditions. These covers, such as those available from Bosch, are generally made of neoprene and

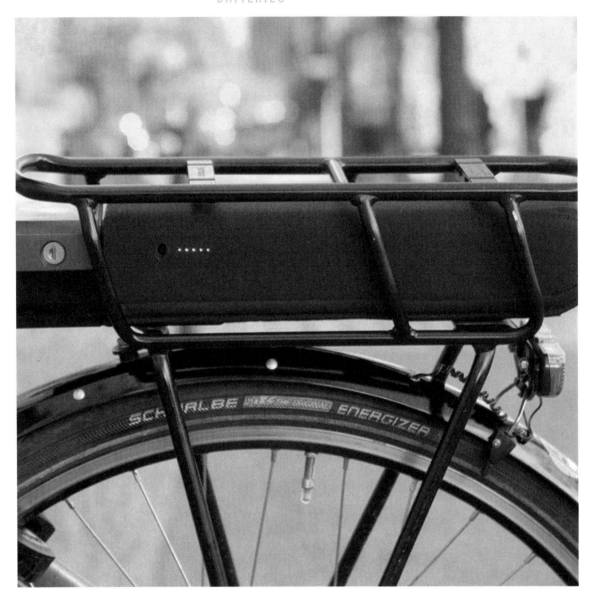

City bike batteries are
occasionally built into
the rear luggage rack.

conform to the shape of the battery case. If the
bike is going to be stored outdoors or in a cold
garage in the winter, it is recommended that the
battery be removed and stored indoors. That
way, its temperature will be above the minimum
advised temperature of 50 degrees Fahrenheit
before the next ride. Another way to keep the

battery warm, especially in winter, is to use more
of its capacity: Instead of always leaving it in a
power-saving mode (often called "eco" mode), be
sure to sometimes set the motor to higher levels
of power. In this way, the battery stays warmer,
thereby avoiding a drop in temperature and
corresponding drop in performance.

Carrying a second battery with you on longer rides offers peace of mind. These types of cargo bags with a separate battery compartment are perfect for transporting your backup battery.

TIPS

CARING FOR YOUR BATTERY

1

HANDLING. Take proper care of your battery. When you remove it from your bike, be sure not to drop it or knock it, and when you install it again, make sure it is properly inserted and locked in place. Charge it in dry, room-temperature conditions.

2

CHARGING CYCLES. Batteries with lithium-ion cells can be charged relatively quickly, regardless of their charge status. The integrated battery-management system, which is part of the charging unit, protects the battery from overcharging. Service interruptions during a charging cycle will not harm these batteries either.

3

CHARGING UNIT. Unfortunately, there is not yet a single standard for battery-charger technology; every manufacturer has its own interface and plugs. Jury-rigging a system is not recommended. Batteries should only be charged with the system with which it is sold; otherwise, irreparable damage can occur, or the warranty could be voided.

4

BATTERY STORAGE. If a battery is going to be stored over a long period of time, it should not be fully charged. The ideal charge level for longer storage is between approximately 30 and 60 percent, which can be seen on the bike's display or the diode reading directly on the battery.

5

WINTER USE. There is nothing wrong with using an e-bike in winter, but the battery should not be allowed to become very cold. Use specially designed battery and down tube covers to keep the battery a little warmer. For longer breaks and overnight storage, the battery should be removed and kept in a warm room.

BUYING ADVICE FROM THE EXPERTS

SURE, YOU CAN BUY BICYCLES ONLINE OR AT A BIG BOX SPORTS STORE. HOWEVER, TO TRULY FIND THE RIGHT E-BIKE FOR YOU—ESPECIALLY WHEN YOU'RE NEW TO E-BIKING—GETTING ASSISTANCE FROM A CERTIFIED BICYCLE DEALER IS A FAR BETTER CHOICE.

TEXT & PHOTOS: MARTIN HÄUSSERMANN

Every day, our world becomes a little more digitized. The enormous growth of Amazon, eBay, and other online stores bears witness to the drastically different way people now shop, a clear transition from traditional retail to online commerce. So why should a person not purchase an e-bike online, especially when there are always tempting offers and seemingly lower prices? If one were to ask the average bicycle shop owner, she or he could expect to hear a tirade about the internet and online dealers. One owner of a bike shop, Uwe Maier, reacts calmly to the question: "Of course you can buy an e-bike over the internet, but you need to be extremely well informed and know exactly what you need and want." He questions the internet model, saying: "A customer benefits from a dealer's role as knowledgeable consultant and from our customer service. You don't get that on the internet." That means taking the opportunity handed to you via well-trained staff, including skilled mechanics, who can take a bike from the showroom floor and adapt it to your needs.

Maier asks customers about their preferences, budget, and cycling experience. Such personalized consulting, including taking body measurements for a proper bike fit, takes a good deal of time, but it's well worth it. Consider the following 10 questions and be sure to discuss them with the staff at any e-bike shop you visit. You'll end up knowing more about what kind of bike is right for you, and after even only a day or two of riding the new bike, you'll likely agree that buying a bike directly from a shop gives you added confidence in your choice.

The attention given to an e-bike customer in the shop, along with shop staff knowledge and advice, is invaluable.

10 QUESTIONS AWAY FROM THE RIGHT BIKE

1

TELL US ABOUT YOURSELF. Height, weight, occupation, and so forth. Knowing a person's height and inseam is needed to determine an appropriate frame size. Weight is also important because a bicycle's capacity, as set by the manufacturer, cannot be exceeded. For most customers, a bike with a weight capacity of 265 pounds is sufficient, though sometimes a customer requires more. Determining occupation is important not as it relates to income, but whether the customer is active via manual labor or instead sits at a desk.

2

HOW ATHLETIC ARE YOU? That helps us assess a client's fitness level and physiology. Do you exercise regularly, perhaps cycling, running, or walking? In the end, it wouldn't make a lot of sense to encourage a sedentary person to purchase a high-performance road e-bike when the motivation to purchase an e-bike is to improve baseline physical fitness.

3

WHAT'S YOUR CURRENT BIKE LIKE? When customers come into the shop with their current bicycle, it provides a lot of information. Many customers simply want an electrically assisted version of what they already have. In addition, customers can point out what they like about their current bike, what they would change about it, and what kind of problems they have had with it.

4

WHY DO YOU WANT A NEW BIKE? The question of motive is an important part of the assessment. The answer enables you and shop staff to determine the ideal type of bicycle as well as a suitable level of quality. Many customers might say that their neighbor or colleague has purchased an e-bike and that they would like to get something at least as good. But you must choose the bike with the right features for you.

5

HOW MUCH DO YOU RIDE YOUR CURRENT BIKE? The answer establishes an important benchmark, especially with regard to components and price level. Additionally, ask yourself whether you want to continue cycling at your current level or set loftier goals, perhaps to get in better shape or ride stronger and farther than you ever have.

6

HOW LONG IS YOUR AVERAGE RIDE? With this answer, we can draw conclusions not only regarding bike shape, fit, and ergonomics, but also what capacity a battery should have. For many, a half-hour ride is long enough, while others can ride four hours at a time.

7

WHAT WILL YOU USE THE BICYCLE FOR AND ON WHAT TYPE OF TERRAIN? Identifying your usual terrain and purpose will further guide you in selecting the right type of bike, electric transmission, tires, and drivetrain. Shop staff will know which bikes match your specific interests.

8

HOW MUCH ARE YOU HOPING TO SPEND ON YOUR E-BIKE? You may be wondering why we wait this long to ask this question. It's important to first know the needs of the customer, avoiding the temptation to force a search for the right bike into a price context, since the needs of the customer often don't fit into her or his budget. At this point, it will be pretty clear to shop staff what a bike that meets your needs will cost or what features would need to be sacrificed in order to stay within the original budget. I consider that to be a more honest way of finding a price range than simply presenting the customer with a bike that hits a certain price point but doesn't make the customer happy. Many people are ready to pay more than planned, as long as the end result is positive.

No matter what kind
of cyclist you are,
just enjoy the ride.

9

**DO YOU HAVE ANY PHYSICAL AILMENTS
OR RESTRICTIONS THAT DON'T HAVE
ANYTHING TO DO WITH RIDING A BIKE?**
At this point, you'll have already determined
the most important physical measurements,
such as inseam and frame size, and the staff
will have presented one or two well-suited bikes
for you. But when you have, say, a shoulder, hip,
or knee problem, you can address it in the bike
fit . . . for example, by adjusting the saddle,
seat post, handlebar, grips, stem, or pedals.

10

**DO YOU CURRENTLY EXPERIENCE ANY
DISCOMFORT WHILE RIDING A BIKE?** If
your hands go numb while riding or if you find it
hard to stay comfortable in a seated position, shop
staff can take that into consideration with overall
geometry as well as by fine-tuning the position.
(And that is why it is helpful to bring your current
bike to the store.) Then, longer test rides on the
initially selected e-bike become important. This is
how you can sort out the right bicycle as well as
determine the adjustments that make it suitable
for purchase. You might need a saddle, bike stem,
or handlebar not offered on the bike but that the
shop can easily install, making your e-bike even
more custom-fitted to your body and your needs.

PERSONALIZE YOUR E-BIKE CHOICE

AS YOU LEARN ABOUT YOUR E-BIKE OPTIONS, REMEMBER THE NUTS AND BOLTS SUCH AS PRICE AND FUNCTIONALITY. TAKING THE TIME TO CONSIDER THESE POINTS WILL BRING YOU TO THE E-BIKE THAT'S BEST SUITED FOR YOU.

TEXT: MARTIN HÄUSSERMANN & ANDY READ

PRICE

As a rule of thumb, you can expect to pay two and a half times more for an e-bike than for a bike without electric power. Prices start at approximately $1,500, and depending on desired comfort and performance features, as well as components, the price can increase quite quickly. E-bikes that cost around $5,500 now belong to the mid-range price category, while top e-bikes can cost twice that much.

COMFORT AND SAFETY

It is rare that an e-bike is sold without a suspension fork (with the exception of road bikes and lightweight city bikes). That is not only to ensure a cyclist's comfort when riding; it also makes riding safer because it ensures the front wheel maintains traction even over bumpy terrain. Comfort-conscious riders and those with back problems often appreciate either full suspension or at least suspension in the seat post. Given the higher average speeds at which e-bikes travel, high performance brakes are preferable— ideally hydraulic disc brakes. A strong frame and correspondingly durable, high-performance components (for example, e-bike-specific chains or drive belts) raise the price of an e-bike but

ensure drivetrain reliability. Everyday riders should also add on a quality bike light system, including a bright headlight. Especially good headlights now offer a daylight mode combined with a sensor that determines conditions of darkness and increases brightness. With the touch of a button, one can even implement a bright, high-beam setting. If you ride at dusk, dawn, or night, it's important to see and to be seen.

RANGE

Similar to the way a car's range of travel is based on a full tank of gas, battery range—or mileage capacity—is an important consideration in buying an e-bike. The issue of range is one of the most common questions raised by potential e-bike customers. In optimal conditions, a 500 W battery should take you at least 60 miles (about 100 kilometers), though optimal conditions are rarely a reality. Rider's weight, style of riding, terrain, wind, and tire pressure all influence range. Some bike shops and manufacturers, including Bosch and Haibike, offer calculators to estimate your bike's range based on these and other factors. You'll be able to learn how far your particular bike and battery will take you considering these and other aspects of your ride.

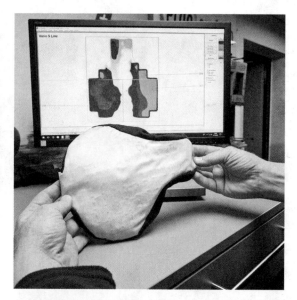

A professional bike fitting, including saddle analysis and selection, can make your bike perfectly comfortable for every ride.

TIRES

This is where there are more similarities to cars. The importance of the role that tires play in bicycle performance—especially e-bike performance—is often quite underestimated. Tire condition and quality, air pressure, and rolling resistance all influence the ride experience, safety, and range of travel. Even the best bikes with the best tires should have a good tire repair kit on board, as anything can happen on the road, and hassle with a flat tire can mean a less enjoyable ride (see more on the subject on p. 88).

FUNCTIONALITY

The variety of bikes you'll see in these pages reflect the diversity of ways you can use an e-bike. You can easily find a model that suits your needs if you do enough research and discuss the 10 questions in the previous section (and other concerns) with e-bike shop staff. Consider whether you'll be using the bike for commutes to work, school, and errands; casual rides on bike paths; or all-out riding over high mountain passes. Match a bike's features to your interests and you'll find a perfect fit.

Be realistic when choosing the type of bike; you may have visions of flying up and down a steep singletrack trail high in the mountains, but if you've barely ridden a bike before, perhaps you're not truly ready for that. A different kind of e-bike might get more use day-in, day-out than a beefy, full-suspension e-MTB. (But don't stop dreaming—just develop your skills and fitness so one day you *will* cruise that trail.)

BIKE LIFE

NEW FRONTIERS
DIY
TIRES
NAVIGATION
TRANSPORTATION
E-BIKE ABS
ACCESSORIES
RIDING SKILLS

NEW FRONTIERS

E-BIKES OPEN DOORS OF OPPORTUNITY

FOR MANY, HAVING THE ASSISTANCE OF AN ELECTRIC MOTOR MAKES A WORLD OF DIFFERENCE. THE E-BIKE CAN GIVE A RIDER A NEW CHANCE AT STAYING ACTIVE, OR IT CAN BECOME AN ALTERNATIVE TO A GASOLINE-BURNING, EMISSIONS-PRODUCING CAR. THE E-BIKERS FEATURED HERE WOULD SAY THEIR LIVES ARE CLEARLY BETTER WITH AN E-BIKE.

TEXT: LENNARD ZINN, ROB JONES & MORGAN LOMMELE

A LIFELONG CYCLIST FINDS NEW LIFE IN AN E-BIKE

LENNARD ZINN; PHOTOS BY BRAD KAMINSKI

About seven years ago, I developed a heart arrhythmia—an irregular heart rhythm caused by electrical problems in the heart. I've been coming to terms with it ever since. As a lifelong cyclist, the diagnosis placed me at a crossroads. Cycling (and cross-country skiing) is not only how I defined myself, how I challenged myself, and how I stayed fit—it also was my primary, and sometimes only, social outlet. Training with friends, going to races and racing with them, and guiding bike tours in Italy enhanced my life and reduced the isolation of my work, while bringing me a feeling of success and accomplishment.

Since I generally cannot ride or ski with others without going into cardiac arrhythmia anymore, these sports, which had comprised almost my entire social life, had become solitary pursuits during which I carefully monitor my energy expenditure to prevent my heart from going haywire. I have a wonderful family and a great life, but not riding and skiing in the mountains with friends left a void.

Before becoming an all-too-regular cardiac patient, I had ridden e-bikes a lot at industry events and demonstrations. (I'm a cycling journalist, book author, and bike designer and builder.) I even had owned a couple of them, both with rear hub motors, over the years, one of which I used as a shuttle vehicle for whitewater kayaking and the other I loaned to one of my daughters for a year as her commuting vehicle. However, I had never seen myself as a e-bike rider until my heart arrhythmia got to the point that I could not ride up any of the gorgeous climbs we have here in Boulder, Colorado, without my heart rate shooting up uncontrollably.

That all changed after discussing with Bosch the possibility of building a custom titanium road frame incorporating a Bosch motor and battery. I had ridden this system a lot and found its mid-bike placement, its high torque and long battery life, and its smooth, quiet operation to be very promising. It took some time and persistence on both ends to complete our agreement, as Bosch had not yet authorized any small-scale frame builders to use its pedal-assist systems.

When faced with health issues, Lennard Zinn's embrace of e-biking allowed him to continue on in his favorite sport.

During those months of designing and planning my e-bike, I had another unsuccessful operation on my heart, and my arrhythmia seemed to have only gotten worse. The value an e-bike could offer to me meant even more.

I built my first custom titanium e-bike in 2017 and immediately rode it more than any of my other bikes—I've ridden it almost exclusively, in fact.

The e-bike has been life-changing, as it gave back to me the mountain riding and group riding that I'd been missing. Without the e-bike, I would have been completely grounded at home or creeping along in my lowest gear on one of my other bikes when my heart is sensitive. With the e-bike, I can still go riding while keeping the intensity low and minimizing arrhythmia incidents. Better yet, if I go into arrhythmia, I can put the bike in turbo mode and get home over hill and dale with a minimum of effort, keeping my heart rate as low as I need it to be—bringing it down to about 70 bpm—while the Bosch motor puts out 275 percent as much power as I do. Without the motor, I would either have to ride extremely slow and stop every time my heart rate spiked or I would have to call somebody to come and take me home.

Lennard enjoys long rides on an e-bike, perhaps heightened by the satisfaction that he built his own bike.

Zinn, a professional bike designer and builder, customized the e-bike for performance and fit.

The freedom my e-bike provides—to know that I can always get home if I have a heart problem—is worth an enormous amount to me.

For many years, I'd organized an annual "Zinn Fondo" ride with a large group of friends every year on my birthday in late June. It was famous for how long and hard it was. We rode from first light into the dark on one of the longest days of the year—generally around 200 miles with around 20,000 feet of climbing, often including a lot of dirt sections as well.

I used to love long, hard, all-day rides like that. Fortunately, the 85-mile range of the Bosch system with a 500 Wh battery on my e-bike makes it possible for me to once again join at least a portion of the epic rides undertaken by my buddies. I recently rode with about 20 friends up an unpaved, car-free road in Rocky Mountain National Park and then over and down Trail Ridge Road, the highest continuous paved road in the US, topping out at 12,182 feet (3,713 meters). It had been five years to the day since I was up over the top of Trail Ridge Road—I was riding my bike home to Boulder from Steamboat Springs that day, a great, 200-mile solo ride. A couple of weeks later, I did an epic (and final) Zinn Fondo, also riding from dawn to dusk and over very high passes, lots of it on dirt. Those were the last long, hard rides ever for me, as a month later I had my first heart arrhythmia, and I haven't been able to do anything of the sort since.

I didn't miss pushing my body hard to get up over 12,000 feet. I thoroughly enjoyed riding up with minimal effort, not even breaking a sweat (since I have to keep my heart rate from getting to 110 bpm). I completely enjoyed the entire experience, riding with a couple of friends going at a good pace, and I even took the time to talk to others and offer assistance where needed (I had enough extra battery power to push a buddy with serious leg cramps up the last section to the top), and I only needed a couple of sips from my water bottle. To get to the visitor's center at the top of the unpaved climb and not be tired, hungry, and out of water—well, that's the first time that's ever happened to me when I got there by bike.

I also celebrate the fact that I can again ride the cyclocross courses I used to love racing on for so many years. As this bike has disc brakes and lots of mud clearance for cyclocross tires, it's perfect! Cyclocross was always like being a kid again for me—riding around in the mud and horrible conditions with a bunch of good friends. And I feel like a kid again on my e-bike!

As I used to think of myself as being too big and tough to ride an e-bike, it is quite a transformation for me to be riding one. I'm grinning ear to ear most of the time, and I'm certainly feeling no shame when I'm on it. It gives me great freedom to enjoy all kinds of riding again, including (especially) with other people.

Team Great Britain leads the field on a smooth section of the course.

TEXT & PHOTOS BY ROB JONES

At the 2018 Mountain Bike World Championships in Lenzerheide, Switzerland, a staff member from the UCI (the world's governing body of bike racing) approached Patrice Drouin, one of the organizers of the following year's event in Mont-Sainte-Anne, Quebec, and asked if his group could add e-MTBs to the 2019 event. Patrice recalls, "David Lappartient [the UCI President] and his team approached us about taking the lead on electric mountain bike racing. They asked us if we would be able to implement it in the 2019 program. So, we went back home to talk as a group and see what we could do.

"There was no criteria about the racetrack, so we were free to propose something. We came back to the UCI with our proposal for the course that would best suit the sport. So it [was] a 14.7-kilometer [9-mile] course, two laps, with lots of variation of terrain. It [was] not done for spectators, like the cross-country course design; it [was] more for the participant. The battery, the bikes, the finesse of using or not using the battery to [make it] last long enough were all part of our proposal."

The circuit was modified right up until the day before the women's and men's races took place. The first e-MTB titles were awarded to Nathalie Schneitter of Switzerland and Alan Hatherly of South Africa (who was the 2018 under-23 world champion). Winners received rainbow jerseys with a lightning bolt on the chest.

Nathalie Schneitter
(rear) of Switzerland
passed the race
leader in the final lap
to take the victory.

The UCI set technical specifications of pedal assist (use of throttle was prohibited), a maximum power-assist speed of 15 mph, and no battery replacement during the race. While incorporating sections of the cross-country circuit used for traditional mountain bike races, the e-MTB circuit was designed to demand e-bike-specific skills with very long and steep climbs—steeper than possible for a cross-country race—and long descents. It was reduced substantially from the original 8-mile length to roughly 3.7 miles. Women and men raced four laps of the revised course.

The entrants included everyone from Olympic champions, such as Julien Absalon, Jaroslav Kulhavý, and Miguel Martinez, to local-level riders participating in their first major race.

Absalon was the favorite for the men's race after racing—and winning—much of the season in Europe in e-MTB events. But in the end, it was two younger riders who finished ahead of him, with Hatherly riding away from the field to take the title and give Specialized bragging rights among the e-MTB manufacturers. Jerome Gilloux of France took the silver medal, with Absalon moving up through the field to take bronze.

"My team, Specialized Racing, asked me to race this race," said Hatherly. "I had been overtraining, which forced me onto the e-MTB for recovery, and that really worked in my favor as I got used to the bike. You really

have to be an all-round competitor to do well, as it is a real combination of a cross-country course and a downhill course. It's definitely not as easy as getting on the bike and going. I wouldn't be surprised if it makes it to the world circuit eventually."

The women's field consisted of only eight riders, and it quickly became a two-rider race—former U-23 world champion Nathalie Schneitter versus Maghalie Rochette (Canada). Cyclocross and mountain bike pro Rochette was in her first e-MTB race, while Schneitter had been racing regularly. Rochette was the stronger climber, but Schneitter was a better technical rider and descender, and that proved to make the difference. After Rochette bobbled on a technical section of the climb, Schneitter caught up to her, and then went into the final rock garden descent in the lead, which she held to the finish, giving Trek a win. Anneke Beerten (Netherlands) took third.

"I put a lot of work into this race," said Schneitter. "I raced in three e-MTB races in Europe before doing a stage race, so I think I am probably the person with the most experience on an e-MTB. I'm so pumped. E-MTB is something I believe in, deep in my heart. I see them every day at home; my parents ride them. So I'm very happy to support this great new sport."

It became clear during the races that e-MTB is *not* just cross-country with motors. Tactics and

E-bikes aren't
too heavy to lift in
celebration of a world
championship victory.

skills are different. Rochette was in the lead on the final lap, but after she put her foot down on the main climb and tried to start again, the surge from the power assist caused her to crash, and Schneitter was able to catch her and then open a slight gap on the rock garden descent, which Rochette could not close.

This points to the tactical aspect of e-MTB racing, which many riders commented on. The power assist tops out at 15 mph, and it is almost impossible to go much above this on muscle power. So, if a gap opens on a climb or descent, then it will stay the same on the flat parts on the course, with both the leading and chasing riders unable to increase their speeds on the almost 50-pound bikes.

It also became apparent that all the concerns about battery life were meaningless—all riders reported being able to use full power for the entire race without coming close to running out of battery.

Simon Burney, technical consultant to the UCI, pointed out that this is just the early days for e-MTB, and he expects the sport to evolve dramatically.

"It was exciting to have the first world's, and the start list was impressive. It was so diverse, from four of the six Olympic gold medalists [men] right down to the U-23 world champion. But we are at the bottom of a really steep learning curve, I think. The technology is advancing, and we need to be on top of the technology to stop any technological fraud. The testing protocols were quite difficult to arrange going into the races, but that is only going to get better.

"We are learning a lot about what kind of courses riders like and what suits an e-bike. Riders are starting to understand what an e-MTB is good at, what the differences are over a regular cross-country bike . . . we are all learning more, and I think courses will develop, technology will develop, and I bet that in five years' time, we will be in a completely different place and looking back on the first one, thinking *How did we get away with that?*"

MORGAN LOMMELE

I was hired by the bicycle advocacy group PeopleForBikes in 2015 to fix e-bike laws in all 50 states so that knowing where to ride an e-bike is as easy as knowing where to ride a car or a bike. (See an explanation of e-bike laws in "E-Bike Classification and the Rules of the Road" on p. 46.) At the time, I didn't really know what e-bikes were, but I knew how to change laws, having been a policy analyst with more than a decade of experience with local and state governments. The inputs are the same. And I used to believe the myths about e-bikes, so I was a little skeptical about this work at first. But the myths aren't true. In 2015, people thought e-bikes were motorcycles, and today, because we're actually sharing our bike infrastructure with them, people see them as bikes.

The hand-wringing over myths doesn't matter anymore—what we really need is to shift people's

Slow down, get outside, and see what you can accomplish on a bike.

thinking around transportation from cars to bikes (traditional or not). Few people want more cars on the road. Few people are opposed to putting more bikes on the road. But we are still struggling to encourage more people to ride bikes. A few gains are made here and there, but how are we going to get more people out of their damn cars to take short trips? I believe the answer is the e-bike.

When I bought my first e-bike, my son was 10 months old. I had wanted to bike around town instead of drive, and I had wanted to give my son the gift of getting places by bike, but carrying him up and down the hill we live on was getting harder and harder on a traditional bike. Let's face it, if you have somewhere to go and stuff to bring along, biking is hard. But e-biking is not.

On my new e-bike, I rode around town, but I felt a little embarrassed. I thought to myself, *I'm a cyclist; I earn my turns.* And I was hearing that e-bikes were the plague and ruining our beloved sport. But none of that deterred me. Today, I haul around two kids, groceries, work bags, and everything in between on an e-bike. I never have to drive to get anywhere within 10 miles of home if I don't want to. And I'm proud of it. I was the first parent to e-bike kids to our day care, and now, on some days, I have a hard time finding a spot to park the e-bike if I arrive amid e-bike drop-off rush hour.

I use my e-bike as a car replacement, not a bike replacement. I still have a dozen bikes in my garage, which I ride with pleasure and mostly for recreation. But my car sits around more than it used to. Driving a car is expensive, frustrating, and polluting. Aside from the purchase, the average cost of owning a car is 20 times more than that of having an e-bike.

Let's get out of the mindset that every bike ride is a race or an act of suffering and shift toward biking as a means of transportation and mobility. E-biking is not for the lazy, the weak, the cheaters. If cheating means I'm not sitting in a car in traffic, I guess I'm a cheater. If cheating means my kids see and smell the world from the seat of a bike, that's how I choose to raise my family. If cheating means we're finally shifting from selling bikes to bikers to selling bikes to people who would have never considered themselves cyclists, never would have considered buying a bike trailer and actually using it, never would have ridden the five miles to work instead of driven, I'm all in.

There are the gatekeepers of cycling who will tell you that e-bikes don't have a place in our sport. But it's not a contest, it's not a sport, it's not a struggle. Riding an e-bike is for people who don't care to drive everywhere. Think about where you can e-bike instead of drive and get to it.

DIY

TAKE CARE OF YOUR E-BIKE

A BIKE IS ONLY AS GOOD AS ITS UPKEEP. THAT'S ALSO TRUE FOR E-BIKES. A LOT OF ROUTINE MAINTENANCE CAN BE HANDLED AT HOME—IF YOU FOLLOW SOME BASIC PROCEDURES.

TEXT: MARTIN HÄUSSERMANN & THOMAS GEISLER (PRESSEDIENST-FAHRRAD)
PHOTOS: MARTIN HÄUSSERMANN & PRESSEDIENST-FAHRRAD

Saturday is car-wash day. That's the case for many car drivers, who, between going grocery shopping, running errands, and doing something with friends or family, find time to attend to their cars. Whatever car drivers do, e-bikers can find a cheaper way to do it. The e-bike has already proved, in many cases, to be a great alternative to a more expensive set of wheels. And as an e-bike may not exactly be an inexpensive purchase, it is important to take good care of it. A well-cared-for bike is fun to ride, and worry-free.

CLEANING

Not everyone will ride so often that they need to wash their bike weekly, but ambitious mountain bikers and committed commuters may find themselves reaching for the water and sponge about that often. Cold to lukewarm water is an effective cleaner for general dirt and mud. We recommend giving the bike a quick pass with the garden hose to remove the worst of it or anything possibly still caked on from a recent ride through muddy or mucky terrain. We do not recommend using high-pressure water, as it may cause damage to parts that need protection, such as the bottom bracket, headset, wheel hubs, and, of course, any electrical components.

More serious owners may want to invest in an e-bike cleaner, available at any local bike shop (e.g., e-Bike Cleaner from Finish Line), that can be used directly on the battery and motor cases, battery contacts, and the rest of the bike without the need to rinse it off. Otherwise you can do just fine with what you have around the house: a bucket of water, perhaps a bit of dish detergent, a scrub brush, and several wash rags or sponges. For the environmentally conscious, we recommend using rags that have already served their purpose in the kitchen—but clean them first. Finally, use old towels from the kitchen or bath to wipe everything dry. A thorough cleaning not only allows the bike to shine and sparkle again, but in the process, you may even find small problems or defects on the bike in need of repair that you wouldn't have noticed otherwise.

A QUICK ONCE-OVER

The following components should be checked and evaluated regularly: tires, chain, brakes, and lights. Similar to washing windows or checking the tire pressure of a car, keeping these parts in working condition—or just checking their condition—doesn't take much mechanical inclination. Heavy dirt, but even water—and, in

Wash day: Any bike repair should begin with a proper cleaning.

Anyone can handle cleaning and changing tires on their own; depending on your comfort level and experience, other repairs might best be left to the professionals.

the winter, road salt and snow slush—can clog up the chain. In order to prevent the chain from rusting, and subsequently bringing a variety of other small but important components down with it, it is important to regularly clean and lubricate it. To clean the chain and rear derailleur, spray a light coating of chain cleaner (available at your local bike shop or hardware store) over all parts. Then, use a small brush to remove any clumps of dirt—an old toothbrush works well. Finally, dry the chain and gears with a soft cloth or an old sock. As proper lubrication is essential to a good and smooth ride, be sure to finish by applying a high-quality bike chain lube. The lubricant will also help catch any leftover dirt that may be

lingering, so use a soft cloth to rub away any extra oil or dirt you see. For riders whose touring or city e-bikes use a belt drive, be sure to wash with water only, omitting the lubrication step.

The tires also deserve special attention, as they come in direct contact with the road and move anytime your bike moves. Regularly checking the tire pressure and inflating the tires as needed is not an optional maintenance step. It is a must. In the case of an occasional flat tire, be prepared by stocking up on a spare tube or two and a flat repair kit and pump. Your local bike shop can help you find a repair kit that's right for your bike and your style of riding. Everything else you need to know about tires, you'll find in the following chapter.

CHECKING YOUR TIRES AND MEASURING TIRE PRESSURE BEFORE EVERY RIDE IS NOT A LUXURY; IT'S A MUST.

ADJUSTING THE LIGHTS

Seeing and being seen are essential parts of basic e-biking safety. Both depend on having a properly functioning lighting system and a correctly positioned headlight. In the event that either your taillight or headlight isn't working, start by first checking the wire connections, as these can sometimes shake themselves loose. Generally, the problem can be fixed just by pushing them back together. Since modern bike lights are, for the most part, LEDs, burnt-out light bulbs are thankfully a thing of the past.

Headlights should be installed and positioned in such a way that they do not blind oncoming traffic. As a good general rule, the brightest spot of the headlight should land on the road roughly three yards in front of you. A dark parking garage is a good place to test this out. Otherwise, stand your bike directly facing a wall. The cone of light should illuminate just below the top edge of the headlight on the wall.

TESTING THE BRAKES

"He who brakes, loses," goes the old racing adage. But on the road or bike path, he who doesn't brake is setting himself up for an accident. For this reason, it is important that brake pads always have sufficient padding. You can use the brake handle to check the level of wear and tear on the brake pads: If you're able to pull the handle all

the way so that it is touching the grip, you'll need to readjust the cable, or in the case of hydraulic brakes, the contact points. For caliper brakes, be sure the notches on the pads are visible; you'll also need to pay attention to the wear indicator on the wheel rims. Disc brake pads should have a thickness of at least 1.5 mm. Hydraulic brakes should be fully checked and refurbished at least once a year, a task best left to the well-seasoned cyclist or a professional bicycle repair shop. The same goes for changing the disc brakes. After changing the brake pads or even the brake discs, the braking system will have to be broken in again: Hitting the brakes at a moderate speed five to 10 times in a row should acclimate the discs and pads to one another.

CHECKING THE SUSPENSION

A majority of e-bikes come standard with a suspension fork and sometimes even rear suspension. If you want to maximize the functionality of the suspension, it should be set according to the riding style and total weight of the rider and bike. For air suspension forks and dampers, the pressure should be adjusted so that, when a rider is sitting on it, only 20 percent of the travel is being used up. Indicators (generally some sort of rubber ring) will show how far the suspension has compressed. The so-called sag ensures that the suspension fork is able to decompress correctly, for example when hitting a pothole, and therefore keep the tires in contact with the ground. A shock pump with pressure gauge (often included with the bicycle) is helpful when adjusting the pressure in the fork. Just as is the case with many other parts of the bike, the suspension fork only reaches optimum functionality when it is clean and well-oiled. Multipurpose oils and penetrating oils such as WD-40 are popular among cyclists, but they should never be used on suspension components. Suspension forks require specialized lubricants that keep the internal surfaces slick and protect the gaskets on the stanchions.

BASIC SUPPLIES FOR BIKE MAINTENANCE

This simple collection of tools can handle much of the day-to-day bike maintenance.

REPAIR STAND

Repair stands hold a bike securely during maintenance. They make working on a bike comfortable because you can stand and keep the bike at eye (or hand) level; they're available from Park Tool and other companies from $100 to $300.

TOOL KIT

A box or carrying case with all the essential tools for bike repair will keep things organized and at the ready.

Coarse- and soft-bristle brushes

Old toothbrush

Wash rags

Sponges

E-bike cleaning spray

Disc brake cleaner

All-purpose bike lube

Penetrating oil (e.g., WD-40)

Hand tools

Tire lever

Tire repair kit

Pump

TIRES

WHERE THE RUBBER MEETS THE ROAD

THE TIRE IS THE CONNECTION BETWEEN BIKE AND ROAD. SO IT'S CRUCIAL TO PAY CLOSE ATTENTION TO THE CONDITION OF YOUR TIRES. A WELL-CARED-FOR SET OF TIRES PROVIDES SAFETY, COMFORT, AND RIDING PLEASURE.

TEXT: MARTIN HÄUSSERMANN
PHOTOS: MARTIN HÄUSSERMANN, PRESSEDIENST-FAHRRAD & MANUFACTURERS

There is a lot going on in that black rubber ring around the bike wheels. Whether Schwalbe, Continental, or Maxxis, the big bike tire manufacturers seem to be constantly trying to outdo each other when it comes to innovations and improvements. That's good news for cyclists all around, as something as simple as a tire change can open a world of new possibilities for riding: rugged tread for terrain, lightly contoured tires for the street—sometimes even tubeless or with added puncture protection. A change in tires can make any road bike ready for less-smooth terrain or any mountain bike adept on the asphalt. Year-round riders get winter tires with an especially soft rubber blend, a seasonally appropriate tread pattern, and sometimes even studs for gripping icy patches.

In general, it is possible for all of these types of tires to be mounted on e-bikes. However, when selecting a new tire, you will need to pay attention to more than just size and tread types. The generally heavier weight of the e-bike requires a more robust type of tire than a regular, lighter road or touring bike. But there is a wide variety of specialty tires to choose from, and they're often identified by some sort of e-bike-specific logo or label; when in doubt, consult your local bike shop. Major tire manufacturers develop their own specialized blends of rubber built specifically for cycling, which promise to provide e-bikes with enhanced safety and grip, especially when taking tight or fast turns. These special blends are also said to decrease rolling resistance and provide improved puncture protection.

TUBES AND TIRES

Cyclists who ride every day or as a hobby normally ride on tires with a "bead," which is a slightly thicker, stiffer part of the ring of tire that gets pushed into the wheel rim when the tube and tire are inflated. It holds the tire securely in place on the wheel. There are two main categories of tire according to the type of bead: a lighter and more expensive folding bead and a cheaper, heavier wire bead, which does not fold. Tubes further differ in terms of size, thickness of the wall, and valve construction. One of two valve types appear on most tubes: Presta valves originated in bike racing and are widely used today. Children's bikes and less-expensive bikes might use Schrader valves. You'll find both types of valves on tubes in the bike shop; it's best to know the type on your bike before you ever need

Tires connect you to the ground. They should be carefully selected based on intended use and terrain.

The "thumb test" is unreliable—you're better off measuring tire pressure with a pressure gauge.

to replace it or buy spares—your wheel and your bike pump may only be able to accommodate one of the two types.

Because even undamaged tubes leak a bit of air from time to time, it is important to regularly check your tire pressure. Despite being a beloved method, the so-called thumb test—where you squeeze the tire between thumb and index finger—is quite imprecise; you would be better served by an air pressure gauge. Schwalbe offers small gauges that fit nicely in any bike tool kit. Otherwise, floor pumps with integrated pressure gauges work well. As a last resort, you could even use a gas station air pump. You'll be able to

measure the pressure and inflate as needed (but do so with great care to avoid overinflating the bike tire under such pressure). This is easy if your bike is already equipped with Schrader valves, but even if you have Presta, it's possible with the help of a pump adapter, which is available at any bike shop and can be kept in your repair kit.

Tire manufacturers stamp the minimum and maximum air pressure appropriate for the model onto the sidewalls of the tire. You should abide by these numbers at all times. In general, the higher the combined weight of the bike, cargo, and rider is, the higher the air pressure should be.

Tubeless systems (top row) or tires with an added layer of special puncture protection (bottom row) offer the best protection against flat tires.

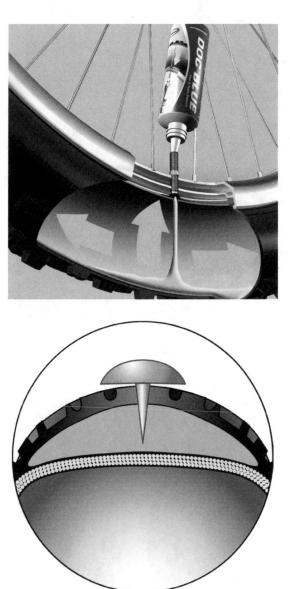

DEFEND YOUR BIKE FROM PUNCTURES

If tires are not properly inflated, they're at greater risk of being pinched right down to the wheel rim when riding over rocks and potholes or bumping into curbs. This not only damages the rim, but it may also damage the tube, as it is light, elastic, and therefore relatively delicate. A puncture could easily happen. Other small objects on the road, such as glass shards, nails, or other pointy objects, can also cause a flat tire. Buying tires with integrated puncture protection can help protect against flats. These types of tires are around 5 mm thick and are made of a special, highly elastic type of rubber, which is placed between the inner casing and the outside tread. This added piece of rubber helps protect both the tire and the tube. In addition to or instead of this extra liner, tire manufacturers sometimes use thin tire belts made of puncture-resistant material. The benefits of a high-quality protective lining can improve the overall ride experience—a fun, worry-free ride depends on having high-quality, reliable equipment. Tires with built-in flat protection are available for practically all types of cycling, whether they're on road, mountain, or tour bikes.

WITH THE RIGHT TIRES,
EVEN BIKING IN WINTER
CAN BE A LOT OF FUN.

OR USE NO TUBE AT ALL

Those who want extra security could explore a new technology that requires no air in the tires at all. Companies including Tannus (in the US) and Schwalbe (in Europe) have created tires that use foam or other rubber materials to take the place of air-filled tires. They're an all-in-one: tire exterior with tread and semisolid cushioning where an air-filled tube would otherwise sit. This system is completely maintenance-free but should be installed by an experienced at-home bike mechanic or a bike shop.

Another alternative to tires with added puncture protection are tubeless tires, which are gaining significant praise in mountain biking and some road biking applications. As the name suggests, tubeless tires make do completely without a tube: The tire, not a tube, holds the air; the design is just like a tire on a car or motorcycle. To install tubeless tires, you will need wheels with specially shaped rims, tires that are marked "tubeless ready," and an installation kit. The kit usually includes special rim tape, valves that will be installed directly into the rim, and a liquid sealant that is added before inflation and protects the tire from small puncture wounds. Tubeless tires have numerous advantages: Pinch flats that can easily happen with a tubed tire are much less likely, the lower air pressure allows for greater contact with bumpy surfaces, and the tires are lighter and have less rolling resistance.

UPGRADES FOR SNOW AND ICE

E-biking in winter can be a lot of fun, but in order for it to also be safe, you need to have the right kind of tires. Many bicyclists ride in the winter using the same tires they used during the summer. That can prove dangerous if it gets cold and wet and your tires lack the necessary tread. A tire made of a softer rubber, combined with grippy, deep tread, adds the necessary safety when taking tight turns or braking in snow, slush, or even ice. One tire specially built for this purpose is the Continental Top Contact Winter. And tire maker Schwalbe has taken the stance that a pure, unadulterated winter tire should have studs; the company offers a studded version in many different sizes. We know from experience that well-inflated tires with studs also perform well on dry streets. Then, when the snow falls, you can drop the tire pressure to expand the tire's contact patch and enhance its grip. If all of this is too much for you to keep track of, we recommend the all-year Marathon GT 365 tires from Schwalbe, which can even be used with the fast class 3 e-bikes.

Studded tires provide grip when winter roads get really icy and slippery.

NAVIGATION

WHERE DO YOU WANT TO GO?

WHAT HAS LONG BECOME A GIVEN WHEN DRIVING A CAR IS NOW A POSSIBILITY FOR BIKES—ESPECIALLY THE E-BIKE: ELECTRONIC NAVIGATION.

TEXT: MARTIN HÄUSSERMANN

Using a GPS service to help us navigate through—or away from—town has become standard operating procedure. It seems essential, regardless of whether we are traveling on foot, by car, or by bike. The good old paper map is certainly still helpful, albeit mainly for roughly planning an overall route, usually at home, pre-ride. But your favorite GPS and mapping apps can find, plan, and track your route and help keep you on-route as you ride.

Take the Nyon from Bosch, for example, which has become a popular, albeit more expensive, navigation alternative to the standard Intuvia on-board computer. The Nyon's functionality is not exactly self-evident, but it is easy to learn, as I found from personal experience. Besides Bosch, other e-bike motor manufacturers have not yet ventured into proprietary navigation product development. But by no means does that leave you without options.

NAVIGATION SYSTEMS FROM THE PROS
There are the GPS specialists, like Garmin, whose products have been successfully guiding people to their destinations for years, no matter if by land, water, or air. Garmin's navigation systems for cycling make up the Edge product line. We

tested out the Garmin Edge 820 and its older brother, the Garmin Edge 1030, which sells at around $599. At this price point, Garmin is catering to a very specific, discerning crowd of cyclists. We found the Edge 820 ($399) entirely sufficient for our purposes, however. It is meticulously crafted and designed with a logical and user-friendly interface; it is even possible to operate it while still wearing thin gloves. The battery life was sufficient for our day-long tour, but it is possible to put the display to sleep if you want to be on the safe side and save power; a light touch to the display is all that's needed to turn it back on again. The navigation works perfectly, provided you stay on the programmed route; re-routing can take a while. The same is true for the "round trip" function, which is in and of itself a charming feature. This function allows you to set a round trip route in unknown areas by setting parameters such as distance and elevation; the Edge 820 takes a little time doing that too. But, in most cases, it was well worth the wait, as it took our testers through new and interesting terrain. Even more affordable than the Edge 820 is the Garmin Edge Explore, which not only offers pre-installed maps, but also a battery life

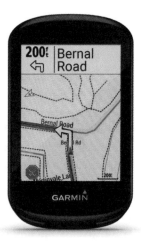

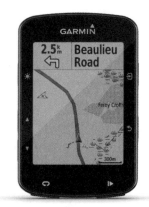

With the Nyon, Bosch has created a navigation-capable display especially for e-bikes (top left). Garmin offers bicycle navigation systems in various price ranges and capabilities.

of up to 12 hours. It has a 3-inch, high-definition touchscreen display and, like all Garmins, can be used even while wearing gloves.

NAVIGATING BY SMARTPHONE

In the age of Google Maps, it is no longer completely necessary to invest in a stand-alone navigation system. A smartphone can easily be mounted onto the handlebars, and there are any number of navigation apps that will

take you to your chosen destination. Google Maps has even been expanded in recent years to include customized route planning for cyclists, indicated by the bicycle icon near where you input your destination.

One drawback to navigating via smartphone is the increased battery usage you'll likely notice. If you are planning on being away longer than an hour or two, we recommend bringing an additional power bank with you.

TRANSPORTATION

TAKING YOUR E-BIKE WITH YOU

AN E-BIKE EXCURSION DOESN'T ALWAYS HAVE TO START FROM YOUR DOORSTEP. IF YOU'RE HEADING AWAY FOR A VACATION, YOU CAN SAFELY TAKE YOUR E-BIKE WITH YOU IN YOUR CAR OR RV.

TEXT: MARTIN HÄUSSERMANN
PHOTOS: MARTIN HÄUSSERMANN, MANUFACTURERS & PRESSEDIENST-FAHRRAD

The e-bike has been so successful because it is a tremendously practical mode of transportation, but also because it promises to offer a lot of fun. But not every bike tour starts from your own front door, especially when you're heading out for a longer ride or multiday excursion. Sometimes, you'll want to take your e-bike to a new destination far from home or use a train or bus to start or finish a bike commute to work. You'll want to be prepared to transport your new e-bike the right way.

BIKE AND CAR

Let's concentrate for now on transporting your bike by car. Transporting an e-bike is not quite as easy to manage as is a traditional bicycle. For one thing, the added weight of the motor and the battery—sometimes 15 pounds—makes it harder to move on and off racks. And some long-distance or touring e-bikes can reach upward of 55 pounds. With that in mind, a common rooftop bike carrier is no longer a feasible option. You'd have to be a professional weight lifter to be able to heave that amount of weight over your head, without doing significant damage to your back or the car's paint job! Owners of large SUVs or vans could opt for an interior rack, or truck owners

could secure the bike on the truck bed. Although an interior system also protects the bike from dirt and theft, it also takes up a good amount of cargo space.

Rear-mounted "hitch" carriers save on cargo space, as they are mounted outside the car on a firmly installed trailer hitch. These racks can often handle more weight easily. Racks from companies such as Thule and Saris are able to carry the greater weight of an e-bike. Check the specifications carefully before using or purchasing such a rack though.

It is worth it to do your own research when it comes to cost, though price should not be your only search criteria. You are transporting very valuable cargo here. Whoever is willing to spend $2,000 or more on an e-bike would be wise to avoid the cheaper, lighter bike racks not designed for e-bikes.

To save a little weight and wear and tear on your rack, remove some of the e-bike components such as the battery, the air pump, or the on-board computer (just be sure to bring them along in the car!).

When shopping for a rack, be sure to consider the length of the tracks on the rack. E-bikes with a mid-drive motor often have a larger wheelbase

The e-folding-bike can be stored in any sized vehicle, from an RV to a sedan.

Car and car-accessory
manufacturers
offer rear-mount
bicycle racks that
are perfect for an
RV, camper, or van.

than normal bikes and therefore require longer tracks (about 4 feet long). Every bike is different, so be sure to measure your own bike carefully before purchasing anything.

BIKES AND RVS

Hitch carriers lend themselves well to small RVs and vans, such as the Ford Transit or Mercedes Sprinter. Some vehicle manufacturers offer their own carrier systems that can be fastened directly to the rear of the RV. Often, however, these types of carriers are mounted relatively high, which can make it hard to comfortably load and unload

heavy bikes. It is much easier with racks that can be lowered for access and then raised for travel. The latter is also true for the carriers that affix directly to the hatch, but those require you to hoist the bikes up high to load them.

Be sure to remove any loose parts of the bike (including the battery) and place them in the vehicle for safekeeping and to lighten the load on the rack. A final option is placing the e-bike inside the RV, ensuring that you and your e-bike arrive safely to your destination, protected from wind, weather, and strangers with sticky fingers.

TIPS FOR USING A BIKE RACK

1

GATHER ANY SMALL PARTS. Remove any parts of the e-bike that could be easily lost, especially the battery and special parts like battery keys, which some e-bikes use for security, as well as any removable displays or control units, clip-on lights, and pumps.

2

KEEP IT CLEAN. E-bikes are valuable, and it is important to protect their electronic and mechanical components against dirt and grime kicked up by traffic. At the very least, cover any exposed electrical points of contact with sturdy tape. Better still, invest in a couple of protective slipcovers (available at many bike shops), which also shield against prying eyes.

3

ADD A BACK-UP. Ensuring your bike is securely mounted on the carrier will at least make any instances of spontaneous theft at a rest area much more difficult. We recommend locking the bike to the rack using a steel cable and padlock.

Trailer hitches offer a sturdy carrying system.

SMART STOPPING POWER

BOSCH HAS DEVELOPED THE FIRST ANTILOCK BRAKING SYSTEM SUITABLE
FOR E-BIKES. JUST AS ABS HAS IMPROVED CAR SAFETY AND HANDLING,
IT MAY BE A VALUABLE ADDITION TO CERTAIN E-BIKES. SAFE BRAKING
CAN ALWAYS BE IMPROVED, AND ABS MAY BE THE ANSWER;
ITS PERFORMANCE WAS CERTAINLY IMPRESSIVE.

TEXT: MARTIN HÄUSSERMANN
PHOTOS: BOSCH & RIESE & MÜLLER

We've said it several times already in these pages, and we'll say it again: The e-bike is not just something for fun, it is also a fully-fledged mode of transportation that, especially in urban areas, offers a veritable alternative to driving an automobile. As mentioned in chapter 2, one of the biggest names in e-bikes today is actually an electric group that made its reputation as an auto parts supplier: Bosch. But this German company isn't just resting on its laurels—they continue to diligently innovate and develop new products for the market, something which their know-how as a car and motorcycle parts supplier has contributed to greatly.

BOSCH AND MAGURA WORK IN TANDEM

Antilock braking systems (ABS) have long been the standard—even a requirement—for cars and motorcycles. Motorcycles and bicycles are fundamentally similar when it comes to driving dynamics, but even more so with regard to braking. So, it comes as no surprise that Bosch eBike Systems decided to consult closely with their colleagues in the motorcycle business before they began developing their own e-bike ABS. As they are already leaders in motorcycle ABS, they were able to save themselves some

of the foundational research on e-bikes. Leaders at Bosch emphasized their expertise in the area when they introduced their e-bike ABS to the media for the first time in the summer of 2017: "With the new development it is now possible on the [e-bike] to not only prevent the front wheel from locking up, but also to limit the rear wheel's tendency to lift up through the use of an intelligent system. Braking distance is therefore reduced, and the risk of falling and rolling over is diminished. Assuming a comprehensive implementation of ABS, Bosch's accident research shows a reduction of [e-bike] accidents by up to 25 percent."

Claus Fleischer, head of Bosch eBike Systems, is an avid cyclist himself, and he considers the growth of the e-bike industry a positive development, save for a few concerns: "In order to ensure this new form of mobility a secure, sustainable place in the market, safety for e-bike riders and the environment has to be a deciding factor." Brakes play a large role in the overall safety of e-bikes, which is why Bosch has partnered with the brake specialists at Magura and established a development partnership. Bosch was responsible for the regulation technology and the electronics, while Magura

Safety technology is advancing. Antilock braking systems are now widely used in e-bikes, such as in this model from Riese & Müller. ABS is perhaps coming soon to the US.

The ABS electronic control is housed in a small box under the handlebars. The system requires specialized brake discs and levers.

contributed the company's overall talent and knowledge of hydraulic disc brakes. The result—and this is no exaggeration—is already seen as a milestone in the history of e-bike innovation. The bicycle ABS works unbelievably well. Bosch set up a test course on the factory premises, and the course couldn't have been nastier. The first test run was nothing but nonslip asphalt; the second consisted mostly of crushed gravel; the third, a mix of both.

SAFER ON ANY TERRAIN

On an asphalt surface with a lot of grip, bikes with good disc brakes can slow or stop so forcefully that the rear wheel lifts off the ground. It takes a rider with a lot of courage and technical

riding skill to know exactly when to release the brake to avoid flipping over the handlebars. A wet or sandy road presents a different type of risk. With so little grip, slamming on the brakes can cause the front wheel to lock up fast and slip out from under the rider, bringing him or her unceremoniously to the ground. The e-bike equipped with ABS, however, is completely unfazed. The electronic sensors notice the rear wheel's lift or slip and immediately reduce the braking force, ensuring that the wheel stays firmly on the ground and the e-biker is able to come to a complete stop in a short distance, rather than launching over the handlebars. On the gravel track, after I got up to speed, I pulled hard on the brake lever. As expected,

Without ABS, slamming on the brakes on asphalt could send you right over the handlebars or cause a nasty wipeout on gravel.

the rear brake locked up the rear wheel, but the front wheel continued to turn while slowing down under perfect control—the whole thing came to a complete stop without showing even a hint of instability.

THE ADDITIONAL COST IS WORTH IT

I started both test runs at a speed of about 12 mph. Braking at that speed was entirely under control, especially with the ABS kicking in sometimes. Next, I got a bit more courageous and worked my way up to 20 mph with a combination of pedaling and motor assistance. Even at the higher speed, the brakes took it in stride—the bike stayed stable and came to a complete stop in a reasonable distance. Then, the ultimate test: a track with varying levels of grip and types of terrain, which is a realistic representation of the conditions many people would face throughout a given ride. I was confident, based on how the previous tests went, so I began again at a high speed. It seemed almost risk-free, and it actually was. The regulation technology is so sensitive that you can feel the intermittent braking in the brake handle, without any disturbance to the actual ride quality. It's definitely impressive.

Now, there are a few small areas where the ABS could improve. For one, the ABS control unit is housed in a relatively bulky black box set beneath the headlight; beautiful, it is not. For another thing, the price point is steep: The ABS kit comes in at a hefty €500 (more than $550; not yet available in the US). On the other hand, as with many electronics, components are continually shrinking in size and therefore might soon fit seamlessly into the design of the bike. As these types of systems become more widespread and mass-produced, the cost should also fall. The first bikes with ABS came onto the market in 2017. The brands Centurion, Cresta, Flyer, Haibike, Kalkhoff, KTM, and Riese & Müller (some only available in Europe) were the first to release an ABS-included model, with others sure to soon follow.

ACCESSORIES

FOR YOUR SAFETY...

... YOU SHOULD ALWAYS WEAR A GOOD BIKE HELMET AND CLOTHING THAT IS VISIBLE FROM A DISTANCE. MAKE SURE SHOELACES, BAGGY PANTS, OR LONG SHIRTS DON'T CATCH ON THE BIKE. CONSIDER SADDLE BAGS WITH INTEGRATED REFLECTORS AND EXTRA LIGHTING.

TEXT: MARTIN HÄUSSERMANN
PHOTOS: PRESSEDIENST-FAHRRAD & MANUFACTURERS

It's one more piece of gear, and you might get "helmet head," depending on your hairdo, but the helmet is an essential piece of equipment for anyone who hops on any kind of bike. Because when there's an accident, no matter who is at fault, a helmet can help you avoid serious head injury and even save your life.

PROTECT YOUR HEAD

Helmets come in all kinds of shapes, sizes, and styles. Every pot really can find its lid. Accessory manufacturer Abus has developed the Pedelec+, a helmet specially designed for Class 3 or S-pedelec users. Its shock-absorbing layer is thicker than its contemporaries, and the area covering the temples and the base of the skull is especially long to provide full coverage to these sensitive areas. (Such features are in fact a requirement in some European countries for higher-speed e-bikes.)

Other manufacturers, like Smith, Scott, Lazer, and Giro, have focused on the so-called MIPS, or Multi-Directional Impact Protection System, which protects against rotational forces when the head hits an object. This technology was developed by biomechanists and neurologists and is intended to soften the blow and therefore long-term consequences of an accident. The added level of safety has not yet been scientifically proven, but research is underway. Helmets equipped with MIPS can cost anywhere between $85 and $300, depending on the brand and features.

Whether your helmet includes the latest technology or offers the trusted fundamentals of good helmet design, it's important that the helmet fit correctly on your head. If a helmet is comfortable to wear, you're more likely to actually use it. And it will do its job better when it stays in place on your head, not slipping off-center.

BE SEEN

It is certainly not a bad idea to buy a helmet in a bright, noticeable color. When you wear a bright helmet and some highly visible clothing, you will be easy to spot on the road in even the worst light and traffic conditions. There are plenty of possibilities, from neon shirts and vests to jackets, shoes, and gloves with reflective stripes. If commuters have to wear their work clothing during their ride, they should at least put on a bright yellow reflective vest or jacket while on their e-bikes.

Whoever decides to buy an expensive e-bike should invest not only in safety apparel and but also in a sturdy bike lock.

Ortlieb's saddle bags are outfitted with reflectors (left). The cyclist's backpack from Deuter, the Attack, has integrated back protection (right).

GEAR & BIKE STORAGE

Tying your jacket or other objects down on the luggage rack is only the second-best idea. Best-case scenario, whatever you're carrying gets dirty; worst-case scenario, it falls off while you're riding, and, if it's a jacket, the sleeves get tangled in the rear wheel and cause an accident. Long story short: having a proper way to carry something on your bike is anything but luxury—it's a necessity. Daily commuters and long-distance riders often use panniers that can be secured to the luggage rack in such a way that they don't wobble or create any instability. Even if this sounds like surreptitious advertising, our team swears by the back-roller panniers from Ortlieb. We have used them for over a decade, and they are still in immaculate condition despite intensive daily use. Our red Ortlieb bags are outfitted with additional reflectors to increase our visibility at night. In the meantime, since we purchased our bags 10 years ago, the manufacturer has started using a new type of material that, during the day, looks unobtrusive. But the bags marked "high visibility" are woven using reflective thread so they are very visible at night when they fall in front of any bright light.

E-mountain-bikes and e-road-bikes generally do not include a luggage rack. Riders carry their cargo on their backs or find a "clip-on" kind of attachment to hold on to the bike frame. To assist mountain bikers who choose to wear back protection, backpack manufacturer Deuter has created a backpack with additional integrated support specially designed for this group of cyclists. The Deuter Attack bag is available in a few sizes and runs about $200.

Whenever you take a break or have reached your final destination, we strongly recommend making sure your bike is properly secured. Especially a bike that cost one or several thousand dollars. Using a regular bike lock is good, but for added safety, we recommend locking the bike to something, like a bike rack, fence, or telephone pole. The traditional style of cable bike locks can be easily tampered with, so we generally advise against them. Much better is the stronger, more robust U-lock. If a U-lock is too cumbersome for you to carry, we recommend a good folding lock, like the Abus Bordo, for example (about $80–$100). My family purchased four Bordo locks at once. They were all outfitted with the same lock and could therefore all be opened with the same key. For those who want even more security, Abus also produces a lock that makes loud alarm sounds if someone tries to tamper with it. A motion sensor is activated on it once it's locked. The Bordo Alarm 6000A costs around $170.

E-BIKING HAS
EVOLVED INTO A
SERIOUS SPORT.

YOUR FIRST RIDE ON AN E-BIKE

RIDING E-BIKES IS FUN, BUT IT'S IMPORTANT TO FAMILIARIZE YOURSELF WITH THE UNIQUE DETAILS OF YOUR NEW RIDE IF YOU WANT IT TO ALSO BE A SAFE AND ENJOYABLE ACTIVITY. HERE, WE OFFER A FEW BASIC TIPS ON CYCLING TECHNIQUE FOR A SMOOTH RIDE.

TEXT: MARTIN HÄUSSERMANN & THOMAS DANZ
PHOTOS: KAY TKATZIK & PRESSEDIENST-FAHRRAD

An e-bike is still a bicycle; well-designed e-bikes can handle as such when not under electric power. Still, you'll surely feel some differences—especially when the motor is moving you along. So don't be surprised that your first spin on an e-bike could take just a little getting used to. If you want to feel safe and secure during your first launch, we recommend starting at the lowest assistance level, in an area where there isn't a lot of traffic (an empty parking lot or road, perhaps), and then pedal lightly, gradually increasing your pedal power and the motor's performance level as you go. (And remember, you don't necessarily need to increase the motor's power level on an easy ride, such as your first one.)

BRAKING

As important as it is to get comfortable with moving the bike forward, it is even more important to familiarize yourself how to comfortably stop it. Most riders who are new to e-bikes have only ridden a bike with rim brakes, which are relatively milder than the disc brakes that appear on most e-bikes today. Disc brakes are more sensitive and more powerful, react faster, and require less hand strength. Traveling at higher speeds, thanks to the motor, combined with the added weight of the motor and the power unit, requires more braking power. In order to get a feel for how the brakes will work on your new bike, it helps to intentionally try to lock up the rear wheel a few times. In other words, slam on the brakes a few times. "You can only learn how to properly control a bike if you know, from personal experience, what a skidding rear wheel feels like. If the rear wheel skids too much, simply release the brakes slightly, and the bike should correct itself," says Jan Zander, manager of the mountain bike school Trailtech.

Engaging the front and rear brakes with different force affects how the bike handles. So before even starting the ride, be sure you know exactly which lever controls which brake (right-handed levers usually control the rear). Front-wheel brakes are able to deliver the most braking power, but, used incorrectly, they can also throw you right off the bike. A locked-up front wheel should be avoided whenever possible.

Perfecting exactly how much pressure to put on the brakes takes a lot of frequent practice. Ideally, the front wheel should provide about two-thirds of the braking power. "But it isn't just the pressure you put on it, but also the ground

A new e-bike owner should practice maneuvering it in a quiet place, away from traffic. The motor does change the way a bike handles.

Balance is everything. You should be able to stand still for a while without taking your foot off the pedal.

and type of terrain you're on that decides how the front wheel will behave. Front brakes should be used much more sparingly on slippery terrain like snow or gravel," advises Zander. He also described the ideal posture a rider should have when fully engaging the brakes. Particularly when braking suddenly, "leave the seat and bring your center of gravity slightly behind it. Your arms and legs should be nearly fully stretched, supporting themselves on the pedals and handlebars. Never stretch your arms completely out so you have room to maneuver the handlebar when necessary." Also, only use two fingers to pull the brake lever. Modern, strong disc brakes can even be activated with one finger in fact.

LOW-SPEED BALANCE

Slow rides are also part of an e-biker's daily routine, and sometimes riding in traffic can be as challenging as a tightrope walk if you're going slow enough. Being able to ride straight at slow speeds takes practice; try it on slight uphills that will let you use gravity to slow you down. If you feel yourself starting to fall to the side, lightly push the pedals to regain balance. "Raising yourself slightly out of the seat and moving your body's center of gravity gently toward the front will work to your advantage," explains Zander.

Curbs and broken
concrete are by far
the most widespread
obstacles a cyclist
will encounter on a
daily ride. Approach
curbs straight on
to avoid falling.

MASTERING BUMPY TERRAIN

Cobblestones, bricks, curbs, and potholes are
simply facts of life for cyclists. You can usually
see them in time to avoid them, but not always.
If you want to get past these obstacles without
totally ruining your wrist or your front wheel,
Zander recommends intentionally lifting the
front wheel. The method takes practice: "A good
start would be to place a small stone or a branch
in your practice area and work on overcoming
it with your front wheel. You absolutely must
come at it standing up and with the cranks
positioned horizontally. Arms and legs should be
slightly bent. Just before meeting the edge of the
object, bend your arms completely and lean your
upper body in the direction of the handlebars,

almost like you're getting ready to do a push-up.
Lean into the handlebars. Then, shift your body
weight suddenly up and back. Your arms should
now be fully extended, able to lift the front wheel
up slightly and set it carefully back down on
the other side of the stone or branch," explains
Zander. Important note: if you pull back too
hard on the handlebars and feel yourself starting
to tip backward, a pull on the rear-wheel brake
handle will bring the front wheel back down
to the ground. It's therefore important to always
keep one finger on the brakes. As a general rule,
you should always approach curbs and other
obstacles straight on. A front wheel that strikes
the obstacle at too much of an angle may be
thrown off track.

Turning tightly and safely cannot be practiced enough. Start by mastering wide-angle turns and getting progressively narrower.

TURNING SAFELY

New e-bikes are not only able to speed up and slow down better than unmotorized bikes, but thanks to improved suspension and tires, taking tight or fast turns is also a piece of cake—assuming the right technique is used. In general, when turning a corner, the inside pedal should always be at the top of your pedal stroke (think twelve o'clock). For one thing, it helps keep the pedal away from the ground as the bike leans toward that side. And it places the other pedal in the right place: Carefully exerted pressure on the outside (lower) pedal helps stabilize your balance through the curve. This technique should also be practiced in an empty parking lot. As is the case with cars and motorcycles, where you're looking is where you're going to go. "You'll ride much more safely if you can take your eyes off the front wheel and look farther down the road," notes Zander. What does that mean for taking a corner? "You turn your head and upper body actively in the direction of the curve and look forward past the curve early on. This will help you master even tight curves."

Riding in a tight space with a large group of people helps teach caution and a sense of balance.

STAY ALERT

Caution is everything when it comes to driving in street traffic. All drivers, but especially e-bikers, should quickly assess situations so they can adequately react. When they see a bike, other drivers will likely assume you're traveling at a slow speed. This is especially important to remember when it comes to right-of-way

situations—a driver who does not have the right-of-way, for example, may mistakenly think they can just quickly pull out in front of a slow-moving bicycle who does have it. In short, we highly recommend to any e-biker—but especially those riding the faster class 3 bike—to try to think like their fellow drivers and anticipate what they may be planning to do.

TRAVEL

HIGH MOUNTAIN PASSES
BIKEPACKING IN EUROPE
AMERICAN LANDSCAPES

EUROPEAN EXCURSIONS

VELONEWS TECH EDITOR DAN CAVALLARI HAS RIDDEN HUNDREDS OF BIKES
FOR PLEASURE AND FOR WORK. HIS JOB GIVES HIM THE CHANCE TO RIDE
THE LATEST AND GREATEST BIKES IN BEAUTIFUL SURROUNDINGS. HIS CRITICAL EYE
TAKES IN MORE THAN THE NUANCES OF THE COMPONENTS OR FRAME MATERIALS,
THOUGH, ESPECIALLY WHEN HE VENTURES TO ICONIC CLIMBS ACROSS EUROPE.

TEXT: DAN CAVALLARI
PHOTOS: FRANCIS CADE & JÉRÉMIE REUILLER

Do you kit up for an e-bike ride?

It hadn't occurred to me until the morning of my e-bike ride up Monte Grappa in northern Italy that a full kit of bike shorts and jersey might not be necessary. If I'm to believe the internet commenters, the e-bike does all the work and all I'll have to do is turn a throttle. It's "cheating."

Of course I know better. I've ridden e-bikes before. There's plenty of pedaling to be done. Get kitted up, ya dope.

It's a good thing I did, too, because Wilier's Cento1 Hybrid looks like any other road bike. You wouldn't know it's an e-bike at all unless you were looking closely, and that's the point. Mainstream acceptance should depend on functionality, affordability, and application, but usually it simply depends on aesthetics. We're vain humans, after all.

In that sense, Wilier played to my vanity perfectly. I'm not the type who wants to be seen riding an e-bike, yet I still want to experience the benefits. Don't get me wrong: I enjoy the challenge of climbing and the sense of achievement once I earn that summit. But some days I want the movement without the suffering. And that is exactly why e-bikes have the potential to be the future of mobility.

On a damp and cool morning, videographer Francis Cade and I set out from our hotel in search of the winding road that leads to the summit of Monte Grappa. On the way there, we both decide to test out the pedal-assist motor to see what we can get out of it. On the mostly flat roads, the pedal assist feels like a shot of bike adrenaline; it's a truly unique feeling, and yes, it feels a little like I'm cheating. I turn off the pedal-assist feature in hopes of saving the battery for the climb, and immediately I feel like I'm on a normal road bike.

That's striking to me. The Cento1 Hybrid is certainly heavier than the wispy race bikes I'm used to riding. So I expected to work a bit harder to follow a line and lean the bike over. That certainly played out, but the difference wasn't nearly as dramatic as I had feared it would be. It took a bit of extra muscling, for sure. But it was easy enough to feel like I was on a regular road bike sans motor.

After about five kilometers of riding, we wound through a small village and started climbing. The low clouds above us threatened rain, though the moisture in the air was already enough to test the efficacy of our foul weather gear. I was drenched, but not with sweat. The roads shared that much with me.

Even with pedal assist, a mountaintop rest is welcome.

Perhaps that's why it felt so daring to take my hands off the bars and reach down to turn the pedal-assist feature back on. The button on the top tube, tucked just behind the head tube, isn't the most natural location for wandering hands during a ride. Slick roads soon laid bare an important design notion: controls belong on the handlebar.

When the assist kicked in, it was easy to forgive this shortcoming. The bike lends a helping hand, immediately and powerfully. It doesn't buck you, but it coaxes. And just like that, my face lit up in a smile as I recognized this ride as something else, not a road ride per se, in which suffering is not just a reward but the whole point.

This was an e-bike ride, in which it was possible to reconcile the idea of riding with looking around, with seeing and feeling, with forgetting the suffering part and focusing on the movement part. There was much to see: a field of ibex romping, paragliders circling down to the valley below, and all of Italy's charm offensive in the form of green hills and red rooftops.

The climb seemed less daunting; it may have seemed insurmountable that morning from the hotel had I been on a regular road bike. The rain, the cold, the long climb, the rumors of snow at the top: perhaps that combination would have been enough to keep me close to the café with its warm cappuccinos and copious Italian pastries. I am out now; there is no cappuccino, but there is movement; there is the top and everything in between me and it.

Later on, as we descended through a thick fog, dripping wet and satisfied with the views we had earned but had not suffered quite as much for, it strikes me yet again that I am not on a road bike ride; I am on an e-road ride, and it is different but equally fascinating.

EASILY CONVINCED

When I have the opportunity to test another e-bike a month later, this time outside of Solothurn, Switzerland, on BMC's Alpenchallenge AMP, I know what I'm in for. I no longer understand the controversy that clouds this new(ish) kind of bicycle. I understand now that the conversation doesn't need to focus on purity or purists' impressions of what cycling is or isn't. This is a bigger conversation about mobility.

It is another day that I would have preferred to stay comfortably laid out in my hotel room bed, warm underneath blankets. The day before, we had been treated to Switzerland's least hospitable summer conditions: a cold, fierce rain all day, as we rode "analog" road bikes for hours up and down steep climbs only Switzerland can serve up. Yes, the ride had been fun, but it was a road ride: The suffering was the point, and the finish of the ride was the reward.

We rolled out from the hotel near downtown Solothurn and wound through cobbled streets toward the hills. In Switzerland, every climb is steep—and don't let the Swiss fool you: When they say the climbing's over, that just indicates they have a different idea of what a climb is. Even the flat roads run uphill in Switzerland.

That wasn't so much of a problem on this day. The Alpenchallenge AMP, like the Wilier Cento1 Hybrid, looks an awful lot like a traditional road bike. But the battery is more obvious, as it's mounted to the seat tube. Aside from that, it appears you're looking at a road bike with a beautifully integrated cockpit, sleek lines, dropped seat stays, and high-quality componentry. Vanity kicks in again.

I pedaled up the narrow roads in the midst of the greenest fields I have ever seen in my life, up steep grades. All while chatting casually with

Allow the motor to give you more time to soak up the scenery.

a friend and bemusing how this ride felt far more pleasant with a pedal-assist bike. Turn it off? Sure, the bike climbs fine. Turn it on? You're still working, just not as hard. And boy, you're going fast. We got to the top, and later on I saw a swath of KOMs on my Strava ride profile. (Don't worry, I switched the ride to e-bike status to get myself off the leader boards.) But what I remembered in the weeks following was the scenery, and the company. Green pastures, confused cows, blue skies.

Two months later, I had a different e-bike experience.

The streets of Brussels, Belgium, drove the mobility point home for me. Cobbles, roundabouts, rail tracks, and heaps of car traffic populate the place. I was there to test out Specialized's Turbo Creo SL, and it was the perfect opportunity to take an absurd amount of pleasure knowing I was taking part in the future of mobility while drivers all around me sat at a standstill.

It wasn't the epic terrain that I'd traversed in Switzerland or Italy, but Brussels does have its particular charms and challenges. The climbs

are short and steep—we're talking 17 percent in some places—but the Creo handled them all with absurd ease. Specialized developed a proprietary motor that blends pedal-assist and non-pedal-assist modes into one svelte motion. The ubiquitous jerk forward when the motor kicks in was completely absent—largely due to the smoother power ramp-up—and it was often difficult to tell when the motor turned on and off. I was occasionally fooled into believing I was doing all the work myself. I just didn't have the sweat to show for it.

In a dense city like Brussels, any mode of transportation that doesn't involve climbing into a car makes a lot of sense. The day before, I had driven from my rented apartment to the city center 10 kilometers away. It took me two hours. I could have walked faster than that. It is here, on the Creo, that I understand how important e-bikes are to the future of mobility.

I am riding the future, mere inches from what will soon be the past. I have ridden all over the world, and now, in a street in Brussels, I see the e-bike opening up yet another world. One of mobility. This is bigger than the bike.

BIKEPACKING IN EUROPE

LITHIUM-ION & SLEEPING BAGS

AN OVERNIGHT IN THE WILDERNESS FREES THE SPIRIT. GUNNAR FEHLAU HAS CURATED HIS MINI-ADVENTURE FOR YEARS, AND HE'S RECENTLY ADDED AN E-FAT-BIKE TO HIS ARSENAL. HE'S PROVEN HOW EASY IT IS TO JUST GET OUTSIDE.

TEXT & PHOTOS: GUNNAR FEHLAU

Bicycles have always been a means of freedom for me, from the very beginning. I'm not beholden to a specific route, gas, or even asphalt. I experience my body and soul in time and space, and I can explore my surroundings just as fast as I can perceive them. To that end, every type of bicycle brings a different set of advantages and disadvantages to the table. Each bike offers its own particular sense of freedom. That's why, when it came time for me to get on my first e-bike almost two decades ago, it wasn't even a question. With a motor to help separate the passion of cycling from the pain (that is, sweating), I feel even freer than before. Nearly five years ago I purchased a fat bike. This kind of mountain bike's high-traction tires not only make winter accessible again, but also the new terrain of beaches, plains, and deserts. "Let me at it!" cried the little child inside me. Then, when Felt Bicycles presented the its crossover model between e-bike and fat-bike, I was immediately hooked. It wasn't long before I found myself taking the Felt Lebowsk-e for a spin for the first time.

ROUTES TO FREEDOM
I didn't seriously start cycling until I was 14 years old, and back then my main focus was going fast. The years flew by as I became increasingly intoxicated by my need for speed. And it wasn't just about speed in and of itself—it was also about how long I could push myself to those limits. So, I chased that same high all the way to routes like Trondheim–Oslo in Norway or Paris–Brest–Paris in France, and so forth. The demands of daily life eventually got in the way of my obsession with speed, and I found myself becoming increasingly irritated by the overall shift toward upgrading one's cycling experience by forming teams or hiring coaches and spending more on training. For me, it was on to greener pastures: I wanted to be completely responsible, completely free, and completely challenged while cycling. In the US this approach has led to what they call self-supported races: racing on designated routes but doing so completely on one's own power. No entry fees. No prize money. No escort teams. You are rider, navigator, cook, doctor, masseuse, mechanic, and everything else under the sun, all on your own. As the races take place over long distances, sleeping breaks are unavoidable. In order to save time, however, you only end up sleeping a few hours at a time on the side of the road in your sleeping bag.

Riding on soft ground really makes you appreciate the wide tires of an e-fat-bike.

Gunnar mounts
various bags to his
e-bike, where he
packs his equipment
and his food for
comfortable camping.

MY RIDE: FELT LEBOWSK-E

....

Felt incorporates the Bosch performance power unit into the Lebowsk-e (which has since been replaced by newer MTB models), offering an exceptionally high amount of torque. A 400 Wh battery easily enables long-distance travel. The 11-speed SRAM X01 drivetrain works especially well with Bosch's electric unit, as it contains only one chainring on the crankset. The wide-range rear cassette offers a large gear ratio with that chainring: the biggest gear, with 42 cogs, makes for an easy ride uphill. The supplier SRAM also makes the Guide RSC disc brakes, while tire manufacturer Schwalbe finishes off the Felt with a Jumbo Jim folding tire kit, which promises smooth riding despite its large size.

Here a bag, there a bag: It's amazing just how much storage space a bike with no luggage rack has to offer.

BLENDING PASSIONS

Since there were no races to date in Germany that fit this description, I decided to start my own. The "Grenzsteintrophy," a race that derives its name from the word for "border post," is a self-supported race that takes place over 746 miles and travels along the former East-West German border. I reached my destination within six days. In those six days I was overcome with an intoxicating sense of freedom, and not just because of the bike. Self-supported racing awakened the long-forgotten Boy Scout in me: cycling, camping, the forest, campfires, sunsets, and sunrises. Somehow, I had the feeling that things were coming together for me that have always, in fact, belonged together. Suddenly,

everything that I had once considered to just be hobbies, outlandish dreams, and childish pastimes flowed together into one. It suddenly all made sense.

GET OUT WHENEVER YOU CAN

Unfortunately, life can't just be one long vacation. The long scenic tour, super-tough race, or off-road journey just isn't an option sometimes. But you can still find adventure in quick little one-night trips. This is what a successful overnighter would look like: Instead of spending your whole life dreaming about great, long trips, you could simply hop on your bike after work and ride off into the night, ideally somewhere in the forest. Find a cozy little spot and roll out your

INSTEAD OF SPENDING
YOUR WHOLE LIFE
DREAMING ABOUT GREAT,
LONG TRIPS, YOU COULD
SIMPLY HOP ON YOUR BIKE
SOME EVENING AND GO.

sleeping bag, pop open a beer, and reflect on the wonders of life. If possible, you could even set up a small fire. Campfire meditation sure beats daily worrying. Start your morning off right with a coffee and pastry and cruise back down the trail.

AN ESCAPE TO NATURE IN 24 HOURS OR LESS

The Felt Lebowsk-e is standing in front of me. Tonight is going to be an especially great one: my first overnighter with an e-bike. I'm excited to see firsthand how bivouac, bike, bonfire, and battery all get along. After 20 minutes into my ride, I stopped at the last available supermarket and picked up some delicious treats for my night. I continued on my way over mounds of gravel, headed in the direction

of the Loccum–Volkenroda trail. The trail is a languorous mix of street, forest trails, and some steep, angular singletracks. I'm traveling with a good 8 PSI (0.6 bar) in the tires, and it works perfectly. So far, I don't notice any major difference between an analogue fat bike and the e- variety. On the street and the flat stretches, I've been able to ride just fine in eco-mode. A loaded-down e-fat-bike drives just as light-footed as an unmotorized fat bike with no luggage. That all changes abruptly when I encounter the first small hill in the forest. I can feel my luggage and all the "motor stuff" pulling me back down as I start pedaling uphill. At first, it's a strain, but then I turn on the turbo-mode, and wow! The Lebowsk-e just flies up the

No overnight trip is
complete without
a campfire.

hill. It felt more like it was pulling me along than as if I were driving it myself. I have never climbed this hill, the last hill leading up to my favorite overnight spot, more quickly or more relaxed. I made it in record time without even breaking a sweat. This round goes to the e-fat-bike!

I set up camp, lit a fire, and treated myself to a beer while I looked back at my day. I now believe e-bikes and overnighters perfectly go hand in hand. There is, however, one difference between my Bosch and me—I can recharge my battery easily next to the campfire, beer in hand, and the Bosch cannot. It's missing two full charge bars in the morning, while I'm completely fit again.

ABOUT THE AUTHOR

Gunnar Fehlau has found a professional home in the cycling world for over 20 years and has been an e-bike user for nearly 15 years. He is the founder of the Pressedienst-Fahrrad cycling news company, publisher of *Fahrstil Magazine* (www.fahrstil-magazin.com), and founder of the Grenzsteintrophy bike race (www.overnighter.de).

EQUIPMENT TIPS

1

LIGHT SLEEPING BAG. I recommend a down-filled sleeping bag, although some synthetic bags pack almost as small as down does. Several ultra-light, reasonably priced models are available.

2

WARM CAMPING CLOTHES: VEST, PANTS, WINTER HAT. Especially in the fall and spring, warm weather during the day gives way to much cooler temperatures at night. On top of that, your body will cool down significantly after you stop cycling for the night. That's why I always carry a warm pair of pants and a vest or jacket with me. Quick-drying polyester products are a safe bet on the trail, as they stay warm even when wet and dry much faster than down.

3

MULTIPURPOSE TOOL AND UTENSILS. You should never get on the trail without a multipurpose tool with you, and you should never go camping without a good knife. The ideal multipurpose tool for an overnighter has a real blade and a bottle opener. I recommend the MTC 40 from Park Tool, which has all the bike repair tools you'd need plus a bottle opener.

4

BIVOUAC SHELTER. No overnighter is complete without a good night's sleep under the stars, which is why I prefer a bivouac shelter to a tent. It is lighter, protects against rain, and doesn't obscure your view of the starry skies. There are immense differences in price, quality, and functionality, so try several on the showroom floor.

5

DELICIOUS DINNER. You're only out for a short time; don't waste your time cooking all evening. Prepare a tasty dinner and breakfast at home (or at least do half the work at home). You'll save time getting your dinner ready and have more time to kick up your tired legs.

Ruh Dich aus: Take a break. No matter the ride's difficulty, this is still the point.

THE E-MOUNTAIN-
BIKE HAS TRANSFORMED
A RIDE UPHILL
FROM PAIN INTO
PURE PLEASURE.

TOURING THE STATES & LOVING EVERY MILE

THE BEAUTY OF THE AMERICAN LANDSCAPE COMES IN PART FROM ITS VARIETY. TOURING BY BIKE GIVES YOU A CHANCE TO TAKE IT ALL IN, MILE BY MILE, SIGNPOST BY SIGNPOST. ONE AVID CYCLIST DIDN'T LET HEALTH ISSUES TAKE HIM AWAY FROM HIS FAVORITE SPORT AND THE EXQUISITE SCENERY OF THE US.

TEXT: HOWARD BESSEN
PHOTOS: HOWARD BESSEN, BACKROADS & TREK TRAVEL

I had been a recreational bike rider for 20 years when, 15 years ago, I had a major heart attack. Before my heart attack, I had ridden in many hilly century rides (100 miles long) on traditional road bikes. After the heart attack, though, I was unable to climb at all, limited by shortness of breath. I enjoyed biking too much to pass up the fitness benefits and many adventures you can have on a bike, so I converted an old mountain bike into an e-bike, and it literally changed my life.

On an e-bike, I take bike trips with a touring company and ride the same roads, with the same challenging hills, as riders on conventional bikes—at roughly the same pace. I can also join a group of friends for a trip without relying on a touring company. And of course, my everyday riding is on an e-bike; with it, I am free of any worries about encountering hills I can't handle.

You may already know about the basic format of organized bike tours: The touring company provides the bikes, tour leaders, routes and maps, support vans, places to stay, and most meals. All you have to do is ride, and your luggage is transported from place to place. The beauty of riding an e-bike is that you can stay with the group, which might be difficult or impossible

on a conventional bike, depending on your riding abilities.

Touring companies provide bikes to their customers, and many of the major touring companies (Backroads, Trek Travel, Sojourn, and others) now offer e-bikes at no additional cost. This provides many advantages over taking your own bike—you can drive or fly to the tour without worrying about getting your bike there, and you will avoid the complicated and nearly insurmountable regulations about transporting lithium-ion batteries. The touring company will charge the battery overnight, and many of them carry extra batteries in the support van. These can be swapped out during the day's ride, making the problem of battery range almost a nonissue.

My first experience with a touring company was in Vermont during the fall. This was several years ago, when e-bikes were far less prevalent and rarely seen on the road. It took a while to convince them to allow an e-bike (my converted mountain bike) on the tour. They were worried that the bike would be too heavy to lift on top of the van, even with two people doing the lifting. This was a far cry from my tour this year in the California wine country: E-bikes were offered as one of the bike choices, along with conventional

Rich fall colors and quiet roads make Vermont a perfect cycling destination.

Bike touring
companies support
traditional bikes and
e-bikes throughout
the journey.

road bikes and hybrids. (I brought my e-bike, and two other riders used company-supplied e-bikes.)

The tours I've taken have had 10–15 riders. Because (as I'm in my 60s) I splurge and take the more expensive tours that offer the nicer hotels, the groups have comprised many riders in their 50s, 60s, and 70s, with plenty of "younger folks" also included. A huge majority rode conventional

bikes; I'll be interested to see how many switch to e-bikes as they age. These are wonderful people (after all, they're cyclists!), and new friends are made quickly, especially since most activities are done as a group. Touring companies also offer many trips at lower price levels, some in hotels and motels, some camping.

For an e-bike rider to be accepted as "part of the group" on a trip, one must be respectful and

Camaraderie, exercise, and beautiful landscapes lead to plenty of smiles. Right: Bike tours in the eastern U.S. come with plenty of shades of green.

not flaunt the electric assist. Zooming uphill past the group would show very poor form. And, for me, it would defeat the purpose of having an e-bike. I want to be a normal rider, not a racer. I use the lowest assist level that allows me to do the ride, thus staying with the other riders while still exercising vigorously.

A typical day begins with an explanation of the route options. There's almost always more than one choice: perhaps a route A with 15 flat miles and transportation to the destination in the van, a route B with 30 miles of rolling hills, and a route C that's longer and has steeper climbs. The routes are usually designed so that everyone reconvenes for a picnic lunch provided by the tour leaders. The day may include an option of hiking, kayaking, or just sitting by the pool at the destination hotel.

The fleet rests mid-ride. Howard's first e-bike (third from left) handled the terrain quite well.

Attention to your e-bike's battery range is a crucial part of planning an e-bike tour. Newer batteries of 500 Wh or more are great, but they can be depleted quickly if high motor assist levels are used for large portions of the ride. The battery should be fully charged overnight to be ready for the next day's ride. A touring company can provide many ways to ensure that a charged battery is available throughout the ride.

E-bikes, of course, are subject to the same mechanical problems of any bike, plus those associated with the motor, battery, and electrical system. If there's a problem while on tour, it's not at all guaranteed that you'll find a convenient bike shop knowledgeable in e-bike repair. On a self-guided tour, knowing how to deal with common e-bike problems can be a trip-saver. And when you're on an organized tour, the tour leaders can help. In either case, a broken part that's not easily obtainable can be a disaster, unless the touring company carries extra bikes. Currently, tour providers carry spare conventional bikes but not many do so for e-bikes; as e-bikes become more popular, they'll likely get the same level of support.

I have taken tours on my e-bike with several touring companies in Vermont, the San Juan Islands, Texas hill country, California wine country, Nova Scotia, and even Death Valley. We also did a self-supported tour in the Cape Cod area. There are phenomenal tours in Europe, and I look forward to riding in France and Italy. Get charged up and go!

ACKNOWLEDGMENTS

Even though my name is the only one on the cover, a book like this one is always the product of successful teamwork. For this reason, I would like to express my deepest gratitude to the following colleagues: my editor Steffi Jaeschke at Delius Klasing for her almost boundless patience, her open ears, and the huge amount of logistical help behind the scenes. Thank you also to our graphic designer, Felix Kempf, who turned my ideas into a wonderful layout, where every photo found its perfect place.

My thanks also belongs to my coauthors. For example, Peter Barzel, who contributed significant input on the motors chapter. But also to all of those living in Göttingen: Gunnar Fehlau, H. David Kossmann, and Thomas Geisler. They all work at Pressedienst-Fahrrad, without which this book would never have come to be. I also can't forget Bernd Bohle, master of PD-F's seemingly endless photo archive.

And then there are all the hardworking people in all the press departments of the cycling world who worked on this book. Thank you for providing me with photos, information, and test material. Thank you also for organizing prompt deliveries and the fantastic teamwork.

Finally, I must thank my family, who not only support my passion for cycling, but also support me in my daily life. Test bikes had to be unpacked and packed again, put together, taken apart, and cleaned. And of course, photographed. What is better than having a ride-along photographer in the family?

And they say cycling is not a team sport!

MARTIN HÄUSSERMANN

Gears and vehicles have always been part of Martin's life. The journalist and self-described Swabian Martin Häusermann (born 1960) began his career with an apprenticeship as an industrial buyer for Porsche before eventually studying business at the VWA in Stuttgart. By this time he was spending his weekends traveling with a camera and notebook, reporting on local sporting events. Since 1989 he has worked full-time as a journalist—a career that he also learned from the ground up, working first as an intern at newspapers *Waiblinger Kreiszeitung* and *Stuttgarter Nachrichten*. He has also worked for the German Press Agency dpa and the Motorpresse Stuttgart, where he acted as both a writer and a photographer. He has lived and worked in Gerlingen, just outside of Stuttgart, as a freelance journalist since 2001. His main areas of interest include travel, mechanical clocks, and mobility on both two and four wheels.

Additional material Copyright © 2020 by VeloPress:
    Inspired Design
    E-Bike Classification & the Rules of the Road
    A Lifelong Cyclist Finds New Life in an E-Bike
    E-MTB Competition at the Highest Level
    Leaving the Car at Home
    European Excursions
    Touring the States & Loving Every Mile

Published in Germany by Delius Klasing Verlag, Siekerwall 21, 33602 Bielefeld under the title
"E-Bike: Modelle – Technik – Fahrspaß"
© 2019 Delius Klasing & Co. KG, Germany

Translated from German by Mark Deterline David and Catherine Van Halsema

velopress®

4745 Walnut Street, Unit A
Boulder, CO 80301-2587 USA

VeloPress is the leading publisher of books on endurance sports and is a division of Pocket
Outdoor Media. Focused on cycling, triathlon, running, swimming, and nutrition/diet,
VeloPress books help athletes achieve their goals of going faster and farther. Preview books
and contact us at velopress.com.

Distributed in the United States and Canada by Ingram Publisher Services

Library of Congress Cataloging-in-Publication Data

Names: Häussermann, Martin, author.
Title: E-bike: a guide to E-bike models, technology & riding essentials /
  by Martin Häussermann, & friends.
Description: Boulder, Colorado : VeloPress, [2020] | Summary: "The
  essential guide for electric bike enthusiasts"—Provided by publisher.
Identifiers: LCCN 2019049772 (print) | LCCN 2019049773 (ebook) |
  ISBN 9781948007146 (paperback) | ISBN 9781948006248 (ebook)
Subjects: LCSH: Electric bicycles.
Classification: LCC TL437.5.E44 H38 2020 (print) | LCC TL437.5.E44
  (ebook) | DDC 629.22/93—dc23
LC record available at https://lccn.loc.gov/2019049772
LC ebook record available at https://lccn.loc.gov/2019049773

This paper meets the requirements of ANSI/NISO Z39.48-1992 (Permanence of Paper).

Composition by Erin Farrell / Factor E Creative

20 21 22 / 10 9 8 7 6 5 4 3 2 1

CREDITS

Pictures: All photos from Martin Häusermann and the manufacturers, with the exception of cover (front and back) Yamaha

p. xii Frank-Stefan Kimmel

p. 15 www.pd-f.de / Kay Tkatzik

p. 16 www.pd-f.de / Kay Tkatzik

p. 21 www.pd-f.de / Frank-Stefan Kimmel

p. 39 www.pd-f.de / Kay Tkatzik

p. 40 (all) www.pd-f.de / Frank-Stefan Kimmel

pp. 42–43 Vintage Electric

pp. 44–45 VanMoof

pp. 47–49 Pedego Electric Bikes

p. 54 www.pd-f.de / Mathias Kutt

pp. 57–58 IZIP Electric Bikes

p. 63 www.pd-f.de / Florian Schuh

p. 64 www.fahrer-berlin.de / pd-f

p. 65 www.pd-f.de / Kay Tkatzik

pp.72/73 www.pd-f.de / Sebastian Hofer

pp. 75–77 Brad Kaminski

pp. 78–80 Rob Jones

p. 81 Pedego Electric Bikes

p. 83 www.pd-f.de / Kay Tkatzik

p. 84 (top left) www.pd-f.de / cosmicsports.de / Christoph Bayer

p. 84 (top right) www.pd-f.de / Kay Tkatzik

p. 84 (bottom left) www.pd-f.de / Kay Tkatzik

p. 84 (bottom right) www.cosmicsports.de / pd-f

p. 86 (bottom left) www.cosmicsports.de / pd-f

p. 86 (bottom right) www.pd-f.de / pressedienst-fahrrad

p. 90 (top) www.pd-f.de / Holger Heinemann

p. 90 (bottom) www.pd-f.de / Kay Tkatzik

p. 91 (all) www.schwalbe.com / pd-f

pp. 92/93 www.pd-f.de / Kay Tkatzik

p. 94 www.pd-f.de / messe-friedrichshafen / eurobike

p. 95 www.cosmicsports.de / pd-f

p. 97 (top right, bottom) Copyright 2019 Garmin Ltd or its Subsidiaries. All Rights Reserved.

p. 103 Brenda Ernst / Backroads

p. 105 www.r-m.de / pd-f

p. 109 Yamaha

p. 110 (top) www.abus.de / pd-f

p. 110 (middle) www.pd-f.de / Kay Tkatzik

p. 110 (bottom) www.abus.de / pd-f

p. 111 (left) www.pd-f.de / Paul Masukowitz

p. 115 www.pd-f.de / Kay Tkatzik

p. 116 www.pd-f.de / Kay Tkatzik

p. 117 (all) www.pd-f.de / Kay Tkatzik

p. 118 www.pd-f.de / Kay Tkatzik

p. 119 www.pd-f.de / Kay Tkatzik

p. 123 Francis Cade

p. 125 Jérémie Reuiller

pp. 127–133 www.pd-f.de / Gunnar Fehlau

p. 137 Howard Bessen

p. 138 Pam Fritz / Backroads

pp. 138/139 Brenda Ernst / Backroads

p. 139 (bottom left) Marquette Edwards, Trek Travel

p. 140 (bottom right) Russell Grange / Backroads

pp. 140/141 Howard Bessen